Graphic Novels in Your Media Center

Graphic Novels in Your Media Center

A Definitive Guide

Allyson A. W. Lyga
with Barry Lyga

LIBRARIES UNLIMITED

U N L I M I T E D

A Member of the Greenwood Publishing Group

Westport, Connecticut • London

Library of Congress Cataloging-in-Publication Data

Lyga, Allyson A. W.
    Graphic novels in your media center : a definitive guide / by Allyson A. W. Lyga with
Barry Lyga.
        p. cm.
    Includes bibliographical references and index.
    ISBN 1–59158–142–7 (alk. paper)
    1. Libraries—Special collections—Graphic novels. 2. School libraries—Book
selection—United States—Handbooks, manuals, etc. 3. Graphic novels—United States. 4.
Children—Books and reading. 5. Teenagers—Books and reading. I. Lyga, Barry. II. Title.
Z692.G7L94   2004
025.2'1878—dc22   2004046517

British Library Cataloguing in Publication Data is available.

Library of Congress Catalog Card Number: 2004046517
ISBN: 1-59158-142-7

First published in 2004

Libraries Unlimited, 88 Post Road West, Westport, CT 06881
A Member of the Greenwood Publishing Group, Inc.
www.lu.com

Printed in the United States of America

The paper used in this book complies with the
Permanent Paper Standard issued by the National
Information Standards Organization (Z39.48-1984).

10 9 8 7 6 5 4 3 2 1

Dedicated to
Marc Nathan, who made it possible without even realizing it.

Copyright/Permission to Reprint Notices

Contents

Acknowledgments

No book happens in a vacuum. The authors wish to extend grateful acknowledgments to the following, all of whom contributed, in their own way, to the completion of this book. If we have omitted anyone, it is only through our own oversight, and we offer our apologies in advance.

Allan Greenberg
Amy Huey
Ann Marie Naples
Beth McKay
Chris Oarr
Chris Oliveros
Chris Staros
Eric Stephenson
Esther Lewenstein
Irene Hildebrandt
Jan Nies
Jeff Dillon
Jeff Mason
Jennifer Hayes
Joe Nozemack
Judy Klein-Frimer
Judy Walker
Karen Boggs
Keith Taylor

Mark Herr
Michael Martens
Mona Kerby
Nicole Curry
Patricia Valas
Patty Jeres
Peggy Burns
Penny Foster
Rick Lowell
Rika Inouye
Robb Horan
Roger Fletcher
Rory Root
Shannon Resh
Sharon Coatney and the staff at Libraries Unlimited
Sharon Gonzalez
Shelley Myers
Susan Crisler
Terry Nantier

The staff at Will Eisner Studios, Inc.

And, of course, the creators, without whom there would be no graphic novels to add to your collection! Thank you for your kind permission to show your work in these pages, and for the creativity you bring to every new project.

Debbie Drechsler
Eric Shanower
Frank Miller
J. Torres
James Kochalka
Jason Bone
Jeff Smith
Jimmy Gownley
Kosuke Fujishima
Lewis Trondheim
Linda Medley
Makoto Kobayashi

Patrick Atangan
Paul Chadwick
Rich Bernatovech
Rich Koslowski
Rumiko Takahashi
Sara Varon
Stan Sakai
Thierry Robin
Tony Millionaire
Vijaya Iyer
Will Eisner
Yoshito Usui

Introduction

Their characters and stories are everywhere. On movie screens. On TV. In video games. In newspapers. In your kids' backpacks and under their beds and in bookstores and libraries.

And, now, in *your* library?

The purpose of this book is to teach you about other books. Not just any books, mind you, but a very specific sort: graphic novels.

If you've never seen or read a graphic novel (if, perhaps, you've heard the recent buzz on the subject, but have no idea where to start), then don't worry—this book will tell you everything you need to know, from the basics of why you should consider graphic novels, to what their best uses are, to which ones to use, and beyond.

If you have some familiarity with graphic novels, then this book will bolster your desire to use them, providing you with solid evidence of the utility and effectiveness of graphic novels in collections just like yours. Whether you're trying to convince a skeptical principal, parent, or yourself, you'll find what you're looking for within these pages.

In case you're wondering, you're not the only one interested in graphic novels these days. They've caught on in popular culture and in the halls of academia. Every month, *Voice of Youth Advocates* (*VOYA*) publishes the column "Graphically Speaking" by Kat Kan, a renowned reviewer and librarian. Publications like *Library Journal* and *School Library Journal* regularly review graphic novels alongside traditional prose and picture books. Even the "Journal of Record" has gotten into the act: Among its many, many recent stories on graphic novels, the *New York Times* profiled the life and works of the late Jack Kirby in its August 27, 2003, edition. Kirby (a dynamic and innovative writer and artist whose contributions to the medium saw him hailed as "The King" in the comic book community) influenced generations of creators both within and outside the comic book community. One of his many admirers is Michael Chabon, winner of the Pulitzer Prize for *The Amazing Adventures of Kavalier and Clay,* a novel about (what else?) the early days of the comic book industry, at the end of which Chabon goes on record with his admiration for the King. *Publishers Weekly* delves into graphic novels on a regular basis, through reviews and special coverage of the medium at trade shows such as Book Expo America (BEA).

At the other end of the cultural spectrum, there's *Entertainment Weekly*, a "journal of record" of a different sort, which has added coverage of graphic novels to its *Listen 2 This* supplement, a publication aimed at cutting-edge music, video games, personal technology, and more. If the attention of the *Times*, *School Library Journal*, and the like tells us that graphic novels should be taken seriously, *Entertainment Weekly*'s move firmly cements the graphic novel's outlaw status at the same time.

So, why should you care about graphic novels? And who are we to tell you about them? That's the point of the whole book, but first let us introduce ourselves.

Allyson Lyga

Allyson Lyga has been an elementary school teacher for ten years and has spent six of those years as a media specialist. In addition to being a Fulbright Memorial Fund Scholar, she is also the youngest recipient of McDaniel College's Joseph R. Bailer Award for her contributions to education.

In college I dated a man who gave me the ridiculous notion that comic books and graphic novels promote good readers and improve vocabulary. He had pages from comic books tacked all over the walls of his childhood room, and he even wrote an independent project at Yale entitled "American Buddha," about superheroes as a form of American mythology. He had been reading comic books since his eyes could track words and was an avid collector, with boxes of comics filling his floors and closets. He had plenty of knowledge on the topic, but I could not take his notion seriously from an educational perspective. At the time, I was in my elementary field experience placement and had never encountered graphic novels and comic books in my pedagogy classes or in a school library. Needless to say I was perplexed by his assertion. Where was his proof that comic books make children readers, and, if so, why hadn't I encountered research and data in my education classes to support his claim? Like so many others, the idea of comic books conjured images of tights and superheroes, of villains and fantasy, of complicated panels and strange character names. I did not read comic books as a child, and because of my naiveté, I could never imagine children benefiting from reading comic books and graphic novels. In addition, being female, comic books never appealed to me because I could not identify with the setting or the super macho characters. How could comic books make children good readers if they only appealed to half the population?

Fast-forward three years. I am now engaged to that same man. I realize that I am marrying not only a man, but also his comic book collection. I had to promise to love,

Barry Lyga

Barry Lyga has been reading comic books since he first learned to recognize words on a page. His passion for comic books carried through to college, where he was fortunate enough to work with renowned medieval heroic literature scholar Fred C. Robinson on an independent project that focused on comic books as a form of mythology. In addition to writing comic books, Barry has also worked for Diamond Comic Distributors, the world's largest distributor of English-language comics, for nine years, helping to spread the word about comic books and graphic novels to the public.

When you're married to an elementary school media specialist, social occasions invariably involve other teachers, and the conversation inevitably turns, at one time or another, to children's books. It's a topic on which I am woefully incompetent to speak. You see, I didn't read many children's books, and the ones I did read didn't make an impression.

I started reading with comic books and I read them to this day, despite having aged beyond what most consider "kids' stuff" and despite an Ivy League diploma that one would imagine belies an interest in such material.

But I doubt I would have that diploma today without having read those comic books. Comic books did more than simply entertain me and open my mind to fantastic worlds of unlimited potential (though they certainly did that!). They also *taught* me. Good from evil. Right from wrong. And more than that . . .

When my peers were figuring out nouns and verbs, I already understood words like "invulnerable," "interstellar," "paranormal," and "magma." While my peers worked on addition and subtraction, I already knew the basics of the life cycle of stars (because Superman's powers depended on the sun's rays and the Atom could shrink thanks to white dwarf star material) and the rudiments of the periodic table (thanks to Metamorpho, the Element Man and Ferro Lad, a superhero who could turn to iron and who bore "Fe" as his symbol).

honor, and cherish "The Justice League of America" and "Sandman." It was time to change my ways and my opinion of the lowly comic book.

While planning our wedding, I had *Bride* magazine in one hand and an *Aquaman* comic book in the other. My fiancé taught me how to read the panels and explained the process of how a comic book was put together. As I became more comfortable with reading comic books, a deeper appreciation grew. With many comic books, I found the plot was complex, the art was incredible, and the vocabulary was challenging. Perhaps there was some reading merit in comic books after all.

As an educator in my first six years of teaching, I started to see the value of comic books and graphic novels for recreational reading and curricular content purposes. My husband kept bringing home more titles for me to read, and I started attending conferences and meeting the writers and artists of some great graphic novels and comic books. These people were as creative and as intelligent as the mainstream children's authors I had encountered at professional educators' conferences. For example, Jimmy Gownley's *Amelia Rules* is just as sweet and humorous as Eric Kimmel's work. Linda Medley's graphic novel series *Castle Waiting* is as creative and adventurous as Avi's Newbery-winning work.

However, due to the conservative nature of my school system and my own insecurities, I did not introduce comic books and graphic novels to my classroom. Although I knew that comic books would be just the thing that my reluctant readers needed, I could not present valid reasons for their placement in my classroom library. I was afraid that if I bought them in, my principal and school community would be in an uproar.

Everything changed when I got my master's degree in school library media. I felt that I could no longer let fear control my book choices. Fear was a form of censorship, and I was not going to let this emotion become a selection criterion. I had to consider the recreational reading attitudes and the reading skills

Was I better than my peers? Intrinsically more intelligent? No. I was just reading something vastly different, and—here's the important part—*retaining it and actively looking for more*.

Comic books inculcated in me a love of reading. I read voraciously, to the point where I was one of the few children I know whose mother frequently would *take away* books to get me to play outside. My comic books landed me in hot water (particularly with teachers who Just Didn't Get It), but they also educated me in the basics of vocabulary, science, social studies, and history years before my classmates. They led me to discover mythology, then science fiction, then fine literature, all beyond my grade level. They followed me to college, where I incorporated them into my own personal English curriculum (to the delight of one professor and the sheer horror of another). And while I've spent many years studying the finest literature of Western civilization, to this day a copy of Alan Moore and Dave Gibbons's *Watchmen* sits on my bookcase near Milton's *Paradise Lost*. (Unlike my coauthor and wife, I'm not a librarian, so my bookshelves don't necessarily make sense!)

If you're reading this book, then you won't be one of those teachers who Just Didn't Get It. You don't have to like (or even read) comic books to understand their utility and efficacy. This book will do it all for you. And the next time you see a kid reading a comic book, remember this:

He's *reading*.

of the students I was intending to serve. I could have the best, up-to-date collection, but if it did not appeal to my students and their reading levels, then my books would become an expensive collection of shelf-sitters.

In 2001, when I introduced the graphic novel series *Bone* to my elementary collection, I was not prepared for its success. All of a sudden I had boys vying for the chance to check out books and asking to be put on waiting lists. They were recommending titles to friends and asking for graphic novels to be put on reserve. I also witnessed boys talking about the plot lines and characters in graphic novels with great passion! This was something I had never seen with conventional fiction books. Students were running to 741.5 (where I had cataloged the graphic novels) and emptying the shelves. *Garfield* and Ames's drawing books were being overlooked for *The Golden Age Flash Archives* and *Scary Godmother*. The conversation in the media center went from *Harry Potter* to *Flash* and *Sailor Moon*. After they had read all of the graphic novels and comic books in my media center, they begged me to order more titles. I was completely astonished and thrilled with the results, so much so that I had to brag to my principal about the results. Something had grabbed my reluctant readers and the males in my school and turned them on to reading. Since I had not changed my teaching approach, I knew it had to be the graphic novels that ignited their enthusiasm.

I guess my husband was right about comic books and graphic novels promoting good readers. I hate to admit when I am wrong, but I was wrong to doubt the power of a comic book. This book will help you avoid the same mistake.

1

Why Graphic Novels?

Before discussing the nuts and bolts of graphic novels and issues such as how to use them in your collection, it makes sense first to tackle the question, "Why use graphic novels in the first place?" In short, what particular characteristics of the graphic novel make it a desirable and worthy component of your collection?

We pose and answer this question for two reasons: First, to give you ammunition to use when a parent, administrator, or colleague asks the same question of you. Second, to provide you with incontrovertible evidence from the start that you are embarking on a path that will benefit your collection and your students. If you have any doubts about using graphic novels in your collection, this section is devoted to dispelling them in no uncertain terms.

This is actually the most difficult part of the book for you, the reader, simply because we are dedicated to giving you bulletproof reasons to incorporate graphic novels that no one can gainsay. Trust us—it's worth the time, especially if you're concerned about the reactions of others or have concerns yourself. (It's OK to have concerns—we forgive you. By the end of this chapter, you won't have them any more.)

There are three main reasons to use graphic novels in your collection, two of which present strong evidence to persuade even the most ardent skeptic of the efficacy of the medium. The other is your secret weapon—it reflects undocumented but crucial aspects of graphic novels that practically guarantee success when implementing them in a collection.

We'll start with the two "scientific" rationales: "Visual Literacy and Reluctant Readers" and "Curricular Connections." We will also point out how Howard Gardner's theory of multiple intelligences applies to the utility and effectiveness of graphic novels. (See "Multiple Intelligences and Graphic Novels.")

Multiple Intelligences and Graphic Novels

Most media specialists are already familiar with noted Harvard psychologist Howard Gardner's 1983 *Frames of Mind*, the book in which he posited that intelligence cannot be narrowed down to a single IQ test and that human capabilities cannot be measured with a test that only focuses on primarily verbal, logical-mathematical, and some spatial intelligence. Out of the seven multiple intelligences Gardner identifies, three in particular make graphic novels a natural fit for a school library or public library collection. While these three intelligences are in some areas related (at least analogously) to the literacy and learning methods mentioned in this chapter, they are distinct enough to merit their own discussion. Furthermore, Gardner's work is widely known and accepted throughout the educational community, meaning that when you use his theories to justify graphic novels in your collection, you're that much closer to acceptance.

1. Linguistic intelligence: Children with this type of intelligence enjoy writing, reading, telling stories, or doing crossword puzzles. They are good with words and possess incredible vocabularies or might even make up their own words and meanings.

Graphic novel connection: Graphic novels are another genre for them to enjoy recreationally. In addition, graphic novels provide a wonderful creative outlet for these children to create and write their own graphic novels after reading a few as models. Since graphic novels offer these children rich vocabulary and scenarios, their imaginations are fueled by the storytelling, word choice, and word placement in the panels of the book. Unlike a typical book with text going straight across the page, graphic novels challenge those children who have strong linguistic intelligence because the text or story line is interspersed between panels or sometimes needs to be inferred from a wordless panel.

2. Spatial intelligence: Children with this type of intelligence are the visual learners in your school. They think in images and pictures. They may be fascinated with visual games or jigsaw puzzles, or spend free time drawing, building with blocks and Legos, or daydreaming. You will see these children doodling on their work or during a lecture. These children are the ones who constantly draw the teacher pictures and gravitate toward art classes.

Graphic novel connection: This connection is so obvious that it is difficult to explain without seeming redundant. For "spatially intelligent" children, a graphic novel is a physical representation of what is happening in their heads. If you were to take a slice of their thoughts for a moment and capture it on a page, it would probably resemble a panel from a graphic novel. Humans gravitate toward things that give them comfort or most resemble themselves. The spatial learners in your school (no doubt there are tons of them) will enjoy graphic novels to read and also to stimulate their creativity to the point that they will want to draw their own. Pair such a child up with the aforementioned linguistic learner, and you have yourself a fantastic creative team. (See Chapter 2 for how a graphic novel is made, and let the kids go to town!)

3. Interpersonal intelligence: Children who stand out among their peers, who are good at communicating, and who seem to understand others' feelings and motives possess interpersonal intelligence. You will recognize these children as the models and leaders in your school. Everyone likes these students, and they seem to get along with any type of group or situation. They can easily navigate through tough social situations and generate enthusiasm for different causes. They may be future politicians, teachers, caregivers, or psychologists.

Graphic novel connection: Much of the storytelling in a graphic novel is communicated through the visual—facial expressions, settings, sharp lines, and shadings. A child who is strong with interpersonal intelligence also can read nonverbal facial and body cues of others and has strong intuitions. These children will enjoy reading a graphic novel because the visual components tap into their strong sense of people, feelings, and intuitions.

Section 1: Visual Literacy and Reluctant Readers
(Traits of Readers and the Graphic Novels Connection)

In Allyson's ongoing usage of graphic novels, she noticed specific traits in those students who gravitated toward the graphic novels and made them very popular in her media center. While most students enjoy graphic novels, there are three distinct categories in particular who benefit from this type of book. We discuss each type of student along with an explanation of how graphic novels meet that learner's needs.

Trait One: Students Incapable of Visualization

Some students have difficulty visualizing pictures. Visualization is especially important during reading, and most educators and librarians take for granted that all students can conjure pictures in their heads while engaged in a book. Even though schools offer visually rich environments, these stimuli do not necessarily improve a student's capacity to visualize, nor do they create an automatic visual learner. As scholar-practitioners Hibbing and Rankin-Erickson (2003) explain:

> We are surrounded by visual imagery through television, movies, videos, computers, and illustrated texts. The use of images is obvious as one walks through a school. Classrooms in the United States often have computers, televisions, and VCRs. School classrooms, media centers, and computer labs are filled with visual images. *Unfortunately this bombardment of visual images does not necessarily transfer to students' ability to create mental images that support reading comprehension.* We have found that our students who lack the ability to create visual images when reading experience comprehension difficulties. (Emphasis added)

In the typical fiction collection in a school library, most books are made up of chapter after unending chapter of text. A student capable of visualization can approach a work of fiction like the very popular *Harry Potter*, read the story, and generate meaning by decoding that text. In the process of decoding the text, that student imagines the characters and setting, which leads to overall comprehension of the book. Thus, comprehension and the accompanying enjoyment of reading motivate a student to finish a book and read others.

However, for the student incapable of visualizing, those chapters of text are a daunting mountain to climb. The words are just that—words, with no charm or imagery to bring them to life. Wading through such print is a chore, and a painful one at that. It is no wonder that some children are intimidated by a chapter book or any book that is print-laden; their minds simply do not mentally connect with the print. They are so busy trying to decode the words that they fail to create images associated with meaning (Hibbing and Rankin-Erickson 2003.)

How Graphic Novels Help the Student Who Cannot Visualize

So, there are students who cannot visualize. What do graphic novels offer these children?

By their very nature, graphic novels help students who cannot visualize pictures in their heads during reading. Due to the relationship of graphics and text, graphic novels support these readers by providing visual cueing systems that not only balance the text but also help the student interpret it. In some instances, a graphic novel may have entire pages without text, thus forcing readers to decode meaning from panels of pictures rather than threatening text. Graphic novels thus form a comfort zone for these types of learners: They can focus their mental energy on gaining meaning from the pictures (and, thus, understanding the story) rather than becoming frustrated by text that constantly challenges their inability to create mental pictures of the story. (See Figure 1.1.)

Figure 1.1. From *Bone* Volume 1. This wordless page communicates a wealth of story information, all without a single line of text. A student who is incapable of visualizing has no handicap here—the story itself is presented visually. From the first panels with their haunting eyes in the dark (and our heroes turning every which way), to the middle panel's desperate run for safety, to the final panel's shocker, the page takes the reader through the same thrills as any prose story, without the necessity of visualization. The emotions and actions of the story are not abstract—they are concrete and physical. *Bone*® is © 2004 Jeff Smith.

This may sound well and good, but the skeptic no doubt assumes that "reading" pictures is easier than reading straight text and, therefore, less effective. If you believe that interpreting a story told in pictures is somehow "dumbing down" the task, think again. Due to the complexity of the structure of the graphic novel and the way pictures and text are intertwined, Lavin (1998) suggests that reading graphic novels may actually require *more complex cognitive skills than the reading of text alone*. So even though these learners cannot create mental images, the process of generating meaning with graphics and text requires understanding the relationship between the two and how the pictures and text work together to communicate a message or story. The student who either would not read or could not read at an efficient level *can* and *will* do so when presented with the unique graphic novel format.

Trait Two: Reluctant Readers

Some students are simply unmotivated or reluctant readers. They are perfectly capable of visualizing, but they just won't read. As Block (1999) explains:

> These unmotivated students are sometimes also unskilled readers. These students fail to grasp the author's use of details, skip too many words, resist interpreting longer sentences, and fill in gaps in understanding by using their own personal experience rather than information presented in the text.

A reluctant reader lacks the reading skills necessary to construct meaning. He or she might not have mastered identifying the main story elements (through reading strategies such as rereading and asking questions) or may stumble over pronunciations of words and complex vocabulary. Hibbing and Rankin-Erickson (2003) discovered that one of their students had difficulty with comprehension because he labored at decoding. Consequently, connections between words and their related images may not be made, which puts comprehension at risk.

Reading is a complex process, and when a child uses all of his or her mental energy simply to say a sentence or to learn new vocabulary, something else—comprehension—is sacrificed in the process. A skilled and proficient reader employs strategies unconsciously and self-corrects mistakes. A struggling reader cannot do so and begins to feel a sense of incompetence or failure as a result. She knows that she just "doesn't get it" and gives up. These struggling children become reluctant readers or, as Allyson calls them, "avoidance readers." You can recognize them in your media center easily—they are the children who find ways to avoid checking out books, or who state "I have books at home to read."

In the specific situation of her elementary media environment, Allyson witnesses the reading development of her students from kindergarten to fifth grade. Sometimes this is the best part of her job. On the other hand, sadly, some of her students who were enthusiastic about reading as kindergartners will barely pick up a book by the time they are in fifth grade. Not surprisingly, most of these students who become reluctant readers are boys. (We do not want to overgeneralize and say that girls do not become reluctant readers—some of them do. And having a framework of thinking with absolute categories can be an obstacle to good teaching and thus prevent reaching those students who most need our help. Nevertheless, experience bears out that boys tend to become reluctant readers in higher numbers than girls.) The main difference between boys and girls when it comes to reading attitudes seems to be simple willingness: When Allyson suggests a book or booktalks titles, female reluctant readers will at least take a book and say, "I'll try it. I never thought about reading this book." Boys, however, will shake their heads and say, "Nah. That looks boring. It's stupid." If the cover of a book has even one girl on it, forget it! The boys will never give it a chance, even when told that the plot of the story is based on the relationship between a girl and a boy, such as in Patricia Reilly Giff's Newbery-Honor book, *Lily's Crossing*. When these male reluctant readers can be coaxed into checking out material from the media center, they prefer magazines about sports and animals, and read informational books over poetry and fiction.

What Allyson has witnessed in her media center is not unusual and is certainly not unique. In his book, *Reading Don't Fix No Chevy's*, Michael W. Smith (2002) summarizes some of the current research on gender and literacy, which supports the universality of the reluctant reader phenomenon and its gender breakdown. Smith notes that in terms of achievement, boys take longer to learn to read and read less than do girls, who tend to understand narrative better. (Boys are better at general information retrieval, but otherwise lag behind.) Attitudinally, boys not only value reading less overall and spend less time reading but also have low estimates of their own reading abilities and are more willing to declare themselves "nonreaders." Sadly, as time goes on, this attitude calcifies, as Smith (2002) points out: "Boys increasingly consider themselves to be 'nonreaders' as they get older; very few designate themselves as such early in their schooling, but nearly 50 percent make that designation by high school."

As a result, boys make different reading choices than girls—informational texts and magazine articles over novels and poetry, for example—and often choose not to read at all. Boys are also less likely to talk about what they are reading. However, there are some encouraging signs. Smith (2002) points out the following:

- Boys like to read about hobbies, sports, and things they might do or be interested in doing.

- Boys like to collect things and tend to collect series of books.

- Boys tend to enjoy escapism and humor; some groups of boys are passionate about science fiction or fantasy.

- The appearance of a book and its cover is important to boys.

This research confirms what Allyson has witnessed in her students and what educators everywhere have witnessed. As predominantly females, it is important for media specialists not to let their gender cloud or skew their observations or their portrayal of boys and girls as readers. At the same time, we cannot allow sensitivity to gender issues to mask the cold, hard truth that boys more than girls need that essential "push" to develop into strong readers. Media specialists must consider the reading traits of boys and girls when developing their collections.

How Graphic Novels Help the Reluctant Reader

What should you do with those reluctant readers, particularly the boys who just won't pick up a book no matter what you try? These are students who *can* read but either are intimidated by text or struggling to decode text. As with the students who cannot visualize pictures, the marriage of the pictures and text in graphic novels assists the reader during the reading process, making the prospect of reading less threatening. Pictures are really the key for reading success in reluctant readers, and perhaps that is why boys prefer reading them. In their study of reluctant readers in middle school, Hibbing and Rankin-Erickson (2003) demonstrate how students understand "the supportive roles pictures play in helping them understand what they read." They asked students to consider the age-old statement "A picture is worth a thousand words" and received the following among their responses:

- A picture helps me by showing what's going on.

- In my textbooks when they show pictures it helps me see what they are talking about.

- If you look at a picture, it puts more ideas in your head.

- If you have a picture it may take a thousand words to get the true meaning of the picture.

We can apply all of the above statements to graphic novels and their effects on a reader. (See Figure 1.2.) If a reluctant reader needs pictures to help in reading, it makes sense to include them in a collection. The students don't consider graphic novels to be "real" books because of the pictures. As a result, not only do they not mind reading them, but they don't even realize that they're reading complete stories! Allyson's most reluctant readers love graphic novels and talk about them with their friends. If students talk about a book, chances are they will want to read more of the books that generated that enthusiasm and put them in a comfortable place during reading. The result: Reluctant readers become regular readers. (See "What Some Media Specialists Think" for some thoughts on what graphic novels have to offer.)

What Some Media Specialists Think

In Chapter 4 we discuss the results of a survey we conducted with a dozen librarians who use graphic novels in their collections. But we thought you might want to see what these folks think of graphic novels as compared to a traditional text:

- "Well, text books and graphic novels don't compare. Text books are usually dry and relevant to what they are learning. GN are fantasy. GN combine words and text in a format that kids love."

- "The chance for very visual readers to experience the love of reading we should all experience. They also encourage low level readers to read for pleasure—which a lot of them do not do."

- "For reluctant readers and students just learning English, the pictures support the text and provide context and clues to meaning. The stories have visual appeal for kids used to TV and in some cases tell stories that wouldn't work as well without the visual component."

- "Wider variety of choice, genre, medium for the 'visual' reader."

- "Entertainment."

- "They are not attacked by so many words jumping off the page and also the colorful pages. The characters are also ones that they are familiar with."

- "High interest reading options."

- "They appeal to the reluctant reader, and satisfy the interests of our graphic-based society. But I wouldn't compare them with textbooks!"

- "High interest books that get kids reading!"

- "I see graphic novels as providing an additional point of view. Also, they provide supplementary material."

- "I think they offer a less threatening appearance that your typical chapter book. Yet the characterization and plot development are often quite intricate."

Figure 1.2. From *Bone* Volume 1. A single panel with three characters and a panicked yell for dialogue . . . and yet this frozen moment in *Bone* attracts (and keeps) the attention of even the most reluctant reader. The burgeoning swarm of locusts is a clear, mounting threat that makes the reader worried for the Bone cousins. The scream of "WHOOOAH!" as Phoney and Fone run away both communicates the danger of the situation *and* comes across as humorous, much like characters in a cartoon or action movie who yell as they run from an absurd threat. Best of all, Smiley Bone's casual stance, his grin, and his placid expression in the face of danger all act to amuse the reader *and* to encourage a worried reader that this is not a life-threatening situation. Humor, panic, concern, action, and a big cloud of locusts in a single panel: Who *wouldn't* want to keep reading? *Bone*® is © 2004 Jeff Smith.

Trait Three: Visually Dependent Students

Students today could be known as "Generation Visual." They watch music videos, click their way through cable or satellite television, instant message their friends with images and icons, tunnel through Web sites, faithfully follow fads and advertising, and text message (in short, easily digestible chunks) on their cell phones. In his book *Media Unlimited: How the Torrent of Images and Sounds Overwhelms Our Lives,* Gitlin (2001) offers a fascinating look at the lives of our students:

> The average American child lives in a household with 2.9 televisions, 1.8 VCRs, 3.1 radios, 2.6 tape players, 2.1 CD players, 1.4 video game players, and 1 computer . . . among children aged 8 to 18, 65% have a television in their bedrooms, 86% a radio, 81% a tape player, and 75% a CD player.

With all of these visual and audio media stimulating our students, how can they have the attention span to sit and read? As Hobbs (2001) explains, "from our students' point of view, television, video, radio, the Internet, and other new technologies seem to have eclipsed books and print media."

For Generation Visual, static text on an immobile page isn't just boring and laborious; it's practically alien. Children have become accustomed to immediate feedback from their environment and impossible-to-miss visual cues as to meaning and method. Unlike the child who cannot visualize, they can form images from text; they just don't want to be bothered. Unlike reluctant readers, they have the attention span and the desire to follow a story; they just need it to consist of more than type on a page.

How Graphic Novels Are Compatible with Visually Dependent Students

According to Lynell Burmark's *Visual Literacy: Learn to See, See to Learn*, educators should adapt their ways rather than compete. Burmark (2002) posits: "It's time for teachers to take advantage of the way kids entertain themselves today, to employ those same media and the thinking habits they foster for the betterment of student learning." (See Figure 1.3.) Media specialists can best serve visual-dependent learners through the inclusion of graphic novels and employing them to teach visual literacy. Visual literacy goes beyond the presented graphics and looks at the messages, meanings, and motivation behind a visual image. Just as educators ask questions during the reading of a picture book, a guided reading of graphic novels can direct students' attentions to the use of color, line, facial expression, shading, and texture. This not only connects educators and students through a popular and appropriate medium, but it also teaches a valuable skill needed in the twenty-first century: how to analyze the media-driven messages around them. Most important, as Francesca Goldsmith (noted San Francisco YA/graphic novel librarian) notes on her Teen Read Week Web site (http://archive.ala.org:80/teenread/trw/index.html):

> Graphic novel readers have learned to understand not only print, but can also decode facial and body expressions, the symbolic meanings of certain images and postures, metaphors and similes, and other social and literary nuances teenagers are mastering as they move from childhood to maturity.

Like video games, movies, and interactive computer programs, graphic novels stimulate interest—in this case, an interest in reading. The graphic elements attract students, who then willingly read the text.

Figure 1.3. From *Amelia Rules* Volume 1. On this page, we see little Reggie betraying a crush on Tanner. The artwork complements the text, aiding in comprehension. From the beginning, we see Reggie's eyes drawn in the shape of hearts as he gazes on the object of his adoration. Then, amusingly enough, he begins to *float*, gliding on the air as "love" lifts him up! Notice that even his word balloons and letters take on a dreamy, wavy quality appropriate to his puppy love (with one word balloon even taking the shape of a pink-shaded heart!). For the reader who is dependent on imagery to understand the flow of a story, the visual shorthand communicates a range of emotions and sensations without requiring the decoding of text. (Remember, though, that the reader is still decoding the *images* and thus still exercising her powers of comprehension.) © 2003 Jimmy Gownley. Used by permission.

Section 2: Curricular Connections—Budget Your Funds and Get Teachers On Board

Encouraging literacy and getting reluctant readers to bury their noses in a book is all well and good, but graphic novels can do more than simply provide good recreational reading for students. Graphic novels can, in fact, be used to teach at a variety of levels and through a variety of subjects. In Chapter 3 we explore twenty different graphic novels and how they can be used, but for now, let us briefly show you how to make curricular connections with your graphic novels. After all, once your students are happily engrossed in graphic novels, doesn't it make sense to exploit their new-found reading pleasure?

One of the most compelling reasons to include graphic novels in a library collection is that they have so many curricular applications. Using your budget money on graphic novels is a wise investment: As we've already shown, students will love to read them (so they will never sit on your shelves), and with the right promotion (from you, the media specialist or librarian) these books can be utilized in the classroom for curricular connections. Once teachers see the connections between graphic novels and content areas, lessons will be infused with excitement. In his article, "Thought Bubbles: Beyond *Maus*: Using Graphic Novels to Support Social Studies Standards," Crawford (2003) matches graphic novel titles to social studies standards. The national social studies standard can be taught by reading and discussing the graphic novel titles he has selected. Basing his selections on titles appropriate for high schools, Crawford points out how the NCSS Thematic Standard of Individual Development and Identity can be supported by incorporating graphic novels such as *A Jew in Communist Prague* (the story of a young Jew growing up in an era of brutal anti-Semitism), *Stuck Rubber Baby* (a powerful tale of discovering one's sexuality, set during the civil rights movement of the 1960s), and *Pedro and Me* (a contemporary AIDS memoir). The Thematic Standard of Power, Authority, and Governance, Crawford (2003) continues, can be supplemented with such graphic novels as *Maus*, *Palestine*, *Fax from Sarajevo*, and *Safe Area Gorazde*, which "draw on personal accounts of war to develop understanding of the impact on individuals living outside of the United States."

These are just some ways to use graphic novels for more than simply recreational reading. Furthermore, Gretchen E. Schwartz's article, "Graphic Novels for Multiple Literacies" (2002), posits that graphic novels can be sprinkled throughout the curriculum. She sites many examples of how graphic novels can be employed in:

- Social studies, where Schwartz recommends *The Cartoon History of the Universe II* (Gonick 1994) as a title that "can bring new life beyond bland textbooks" with its coverage of Far Eastern history and the fall of Rome. "Although packed with information, the book's black-and-white drawings demonstrate that history can be fun and funny, too."

- English, where teachers can use graphic novels not only for the purpose of teaching traditional literary techniques, ideas, and themes, but also as a way to initiate class discussions that will lead to other, related, works. For example, she recommends using the Victorian murder graphic novel *The Mystery of Mary Rogers* (Geary 2001) as "a bridge to other classics of that period."

Graphic novels can be an end or a means for teachers. They can generate class discussion and lead to broader topics, or they can be studied in their own right as worthy, valuable literature and source material.

Media specialists are the information specialists and literature specialists in their school buildings. Since teachers do not always have the time or, sadly, the willingness to explore current literature for children and young adults, it is our responsibility to educate them and include graphic novels in our collections. By enlightening teachers about the connections graphic novels have to content areas, we expand their teaching possibilities and give the students what they want: learning that is fun and enjoyable. And, of course, *effective*.

However, placing the books on the shelves will not get them checked out by teachers. We all know this! Since not everyone will consider graphic novels "appropriate," you will need to be a little creative.

You're reading this book—you are armed with a plethora of reasons to have graphic novels in your collection, but here are some suggestions to promote graphic novels for curricular purposes (to get them in the hands of teachers!):

- 📖 Go to the team/department meetings and bring the books, with Post-It notes inside showing places where it connects to the content.

- 📖 Throw a graphic novel/comic book party after school. Those who come in costume as a comic book character will receive a free graphic novel for their classroom. (They get two if they show up in tights!)

- 📖 Ask your principal for five to ten minutes at a faculty meeting, and booktalk two or three graphic novels. These meetings are usually held in the media center anyway, so it will be convenient for the teachers to check those books out right away.

- 📖 E-mail a particular teacher, team, or the entire faculty about the graphic novels in your collection. Make it a habit—once or twice a month, highlight a few titles.

- 📖 Use the direct approach: Check out a graphic novel in a teacher's name and stick it in her mailbox along with a note saying, "I saw this book and thought of your class."

- 📖 Start a graphic novel reading club at your school. Mix it up with students and teachers.

- 📖 Conduct a beginning of the year faculty survey. Include a question about graphic novels. If teachers leave this blank, you have a lot of work to do. If someone lists twenty-five favorite titles and authors, find that person, befriend her, and let her be a shining example.

Good luck! You may only have one or two brave souls at first, but consider each one a victory. (See "Allyson Talks Graphically!")

Allyson Talks Graphically!

In my elementary school, many teachers thought that graphic novels were fine for students to read recreationally but never took them seriously for classroom teaching. What did I do? I checked out P. Craig Russell's graphic version of *Fairy Tales of Oscar Wilde: The Selfish Giants & the Star Child* to a third grade teacher who was studying fairy tales. She was surprised by the book and didn't know how to approach it until I showed her how to use it as a read-aloud by employing the "picture walk" strategy that she usually used with traditional fairy tales. The students loved the illustrations, and she was sharing a rather sophisticated author, Oscar Wilde, with students whom you would not expect to enjoy such literature at a young age. His original text would not work with young students; however, a graphic novel version of his story *does* work and is appropriate for the classroom.

I have also booktalked graphic novel titles at faculty meetings. I have booktalked graphic novels both at the end and at the beginning of faculty meetings, and in my experience giving these presentations at the beginning of the faculty meeting is more successful. After talking about the titles and highlighting connections to content areas, teachers took them from me after the booktalks and checked out the titles.

Anytime I can put graphic novels in the hands of teachers, I consider it a success!

Be sure to look at the appendix in the back of the book, which lists a hundred graphic novel titles with curricular connections, authors, copyright dates, and reviews. Please explore the appendix for titles that meet your school's curricular needs.

Section 3: High Interest and Pop Culture

Spider-Man. X-Men. Hulk. Justice League. Smallville. Teen Titans. Have you heard your students talk about these movies and TV shows? All started their "lives" as comic books or graphic novels and then were adapted into other media. In an article for the *Washington Post*, Steven Hunter (2002) explains how the "graphic novel isn't really a novel; what it is, really, is a movie in graphics. It tells stories visually, finding images to express emotions that would somehow be beyond a prose artist's ability to convey" (G1). The fantastic and action-oriented story lines found in so many graphic novels serve to keep students' interest levels high. Even a "slow" moment in a comic book is exciting because it is visual; the student experiences it viscerally. A conversation isn't just alternating lines of dialogue; it can be lit with interesting colors, drawn with panache, and framed so as to entertain the eye in a way that lines of dialogue on a page cannot. Max Allan Collins, the author of *Road to Perdition* (which was adapted into the Academy Award-winning movie)*,* stated: "This is an art form that is every bit as valid for telling stories and entertaining people as movies or any other form" (Dvorak 2002).

Furthermore, the very format of a graphic novel is completely different from that of the students' standard textbook (which they probably consider boring or intimidating). When you show a student a graphic novel instead of the usual textbook, you get his or her attention immediately, if for no other reason than that it's *different* and unexpected in the school environment. Getting the students' attention is half the battle, and a graphic novel is a powerful weapon in that battle.

Why? Because even for those children who aren't already reading them, comic books and graphic novels have much to offer and much to keep them glued to the page, especially by virtue of remaining on the cutting edge of pop culture. We have all experienced the sinking feeling that comes from realizing (usually too late!) that popular culture is moving too quickly around us. While children seem to have an innate ability to keep up with what is "cool" and what is not, we often find ourselves five minutes behind them. As a result, we end up speaking a different language, alluding to passé or outdated concepts, and generally not communicating (or keeping their interest!) as well as we should.

Graphic novels, by their very nature, tend to cling to the cutting edge of popular culture. They react to social and cultural changes swiftly, often in advance of other media.

One example of this difference in the ability to make rapid changes is the aftermath of the terrorist attacks of September 11, 2001. In the wake of the attacks, TV schedules were reshuffled and thrown into disarray, and movie studios pulled movies from their release dates. It took almost a year for the book publishing and music industries to provide responses to the attacks.

For the comic book industry, the first response came in *less than a month*. Two days after the attacks, Marvel Comics announced its intention to publish *Heroes*, a commemorative magazine from which all profits would go to the families of firefighters killed that day. From concept to development to delivery, *Heroes* was in stores across the country in a month. Shortly thereafter, Marvel published a special issue of *The Amazing Spider-Man* that dealt with the attacks. Other publishers rushed similar charity projects into publication. Only the *America: A Tribute to Heroes* telethon beat the comic book industry to "market" with its 9/11 response, and in that case it was a single event. The comic book industry published magazines, comic books, and graphic novels about 9/11 before the first books hit bookstore shelves and long before Bruce Springsteen could get *The Rising* out of the studio.

Pop culture moves quickly. Children know this. They thrive on it. Comic books move just as quickly, making them an important *and timely* addition in your teaching toolbox. Having them in your media collection immediately makes connections to a student's life outside of school and tacitly acknowledges what is hip and cool, making the collection itself all the more attractive.

Summary

Convinced? Graphic novels are up to the task at hand and make sense for your collection. Now that you know why you need them and have some ideas about how to use them, turn the page and let's figure out exactly *what* makes a graphic novel . . . and what you need to know about it.

2

Introduction to Graphic Novels and Common Terms

Section 1: Definitions

To incorporate graphic novels into your collection, first you must have an understanding of precisely what it is you are incorporating. This section introduces common terms, formats, and vocabulary for use when dealing with this particular medium. (There is a glossary of terms at the end of the book as well.)

The words "comic book" conjure an image of the typical thirty-two-page, stapled pamphlet to most people, but the fact of the matter is comic books come in many shapes, sizes, and formats. Even the terms "comic book" and "comics" can be misnomers in many cases, but they still endure, due mainly to nostalgia and the fact that no one has ever developed a word that encompasses the rich variety and unique nature of comics all at once.

What Is a Comic Book? What Is a Graphic Novel?

In his landmark *Understanding Comics*, Scott McCloud (1994) spends a good deal of time searching for a precise definition of what a comic book is, eventually settling on the torturous (but technically accurate) "juxtaposed pictorial and other images in deliberate sequence, intended to convey information and/or to produce an aesthetic response in the viewer." The reason for McCloud's difficulty in finding a simple definition rests in the myriad forms comic books have taken over the years. For the purposes of this book, however, it is easier (and more effective) to *describe* a comic book than to define one.

A comic book is *not* defined by its subject matter, any more than the subject matter of a book, movie, or TV show defines those media. While most readers will be familiar with comic books for their colorfully garbed superheroes, it is important to realize at the outset that comic books can—and do—encompass the entire range of fiction and nonfiction.

The key word in "comic book" is "book." In short, a comic book is a story or narrative presented with words and pictures, usually in a format that makes use of multiple images per page (as opposed to, say, children's picture books). If you are reading this book and are interested in this topic, then you have at least a passing familiarity with comic books. You may recall childhood reading, or a collection kept by a sibling. That recollection is as good as any specific definition for our purposes.

For purposes of this discussion, the phrase "comic book" is usually used interchangeably with "comic" (and their related plural forms) as a generic term that describes the *medium* itself.

In short, then, a comic book or comic is any sort of literature that combines story and art, whether as an *ongoing series, mini-series, maxi-series, graphic novel,* or other format.

For the first several decades of their existence comic books were published in a simple, magazinelike format that should be familiar to anyone who has ever browsed a newsstand. The typical comic book measures approximately seven inches by ten inches, runs between twenty-four and thirty-two pages in color or black and white, and is stapled (saddle-stitched), not bound. (Note that this is the *typical* comic book. Saddle-stitched comics can be—and have been—larger in dimension and page count.)

This comic book usually follows the pattern set by its magazine "cousins" and has a frequency of anything from weekly to semiannual, with most comics being published on a monthly schedule. These sorts of publications have come to be called "pamphlets" in recent years, though that term is often considered derogatory by collectors. We use the term "periodical" to refer to a comic book published in such a format and on such a schedule.

The *graphic novel* is different. The graphic novel is more like a traditional novel, in that it is published on an independent schedule. It is longer in format than a periodical and typically contains a complete story unto itself. Graphic novels usually have higher production values than the typical stapled comic book–they may be squarebound, for example, with cardstock covers. Some may be hardcover volumes. Although a graphic novel usually stands on its own as a complete story, it is possible to have an *ongoing series* or *limited series* of graphic novels telling a single story or series of related stories. A typical abbreviation in the industry for graphic novel is "GN," usually used as part of a title to indicate to a reader or browser that the title in question is not a periodical.

Further definitions of terms used throughout this book follow:

- **Collected edition:** Another term for *trade paperback.*

- **Limited series:** A *maxi-series* or *mini-series.*

- **Maxi-series:** A comic book series that is scheduled to run only a certain number of issues (usually more than six) and then end. An analogy would be a television program such as *Taken,* which ended after a specific number of airings and after telling a specific story. A maxi-series can have a frequency from weekly to semiannual, but most are at least bimonthly. It is possible to have a maxi-series made up of graphic novels.

- **Mini-series:** A comic book series that is scheduled to run only a certain number of issues (usually six or fewer) and then end. An analogy would be a television program such as *"Roots,"* which ended after a specific number of airings and after telling a specific story. A mini-series can have a frequency from weekly to semiannual, but most are at least bimonthly. It is possible to have a mini-series made up of graphic novels.

- **Ongoing:** Usually used in conjunction with "series." This implies a comic book series that has no ending planned and will continue until sales dictate its cancellation. An example is *Action Comics*, from DC Comics, a series that has been published nearly continuously since 1938. An analogy would be a television program such as *ER*, which runs until it is no longer profitable or other factors dictate its conclusion. Ongoing series can have a frequency from weekly to semiannual. Most are monthly or bimonthly.

- 📖 **Story arc:** A specific story told in an ongoing series over a course of many issues. Sometimes called a *"mini-series* within a series." The story arc will often have its own title, with each issue being a "chapter."

- 📖 **Trade paperback:** In comics, this term is used differently than in the book trade. A comic book trade paperback is a squarebound edition that collects and reprints a *mini-series, maxi-series,* or *story arc* in this sturdier format, giving readers a complete story at one time, rather than over a period of months. Sometimes, a trade paperback may collect stories that are not interconnected but rather are related by some theme. Many trade paperbacks also contain additional material, such as an introduction or foreword, or character sketches. Usually abbreviated "TP."

Hierarchy of Terms

With so many terms used interchangeably to refer to related products and forms, it can be confusing for newcomers to discuss comic books. Here is a quick guide:

- 📖 **Comic book:** Used to describe both the medium itself *and* the periodical form. As a result, all graphic novels are comic books, but not all comic books are graphic novels.

- 📖 **Comic:** Used interchangeably with "comic book."

- 📖 **Graphic novel:** Used to describe the specific format of a comic book that has greater production values and longer narrative. Can also describe the trade paperback format. (For an analogy, imagine a novel that has been serialized, then collected into book form for publication. A trade paperback is a graphic novel that was first published in serial, periodical format.)

What a Comic Book Is *Not*

Despite their superficially similar appearances and their common origins, comic books and the comic strips seen in daily newspapers are not the same. While a complete exegesis on the differences between the two is beyond the scope of this book, the two are confused often enough in the newcomer's mind that it needs to be stated outright: A comic strip is not the same thing as a comic book.

Section 2: Style

Like prose, comic books cannot be restricted to any particular subject matter. Also like prose, comic books employ a wide range of styles to use in telling their stories. These styles transcend narrative choices to extend to the art traits as well. To the layperson's eye, they may include such styles as:

- 📖 **"Cartoony":** Typically characterized by clean lines and representational, iconic images rather than exacting replicas of reality. Even within this category, many subcategories exist, from the deceptively simple linework of Jeff Smith's *Bone* to the exaggerated anatomy of Peter Bagge's *Hate*.

- 📖 **"Realistic":** Probably the most familiar type of art for a newcomer to comics. In this style, the artist forgoes representational images and strives to create a world that resembles our own, albeit greatly simplified.

- 📖 **"Photo-realistic":** The artist makes use of models and photo references to attempt to mimic reality as closely as possible. An excellent example is Alex Ross's artwork (*Marvels, Kingdom Come*).

These definitions are necessarily brief and not wholly representative, as an in-depth discussion of art theory is not in keeping with the purpose (or necessity) of this book. This listing deliberately avoids the many nuances and shadings inherent to each style. Simply keep in mind that there are many different styles, and that each style (and there are more than those listed above) has its own basics, its own visual "language." It is not necessary to have an understanding of art theory to appreciate or read a comic book, but the newcomer should be aware of two things: (1) that there are a wide variety of styles employed in the medium, and (2) that each style has its own attendant strengths and weaknesses. While any judgment about the quality of art is subjective, bear in mind that an artist usually has a reason for employing a particular style, just as a writer chooses specific narrative techniques. The art style used in a comic book may be as symbolic and as important to deconstructing and understanding the story as the dialogue, characters, or plot.

Section 3: Elements of a Comic Book

Books are composed of elements that, when added together, comprise a synergistic whole. So, too, are comic books. Some of the terms below may be new to the comic book neophyte.

In the pages following, several examples of comic book pages are shown to introduce readers to what McCloud (1994) calls "the invisible art," that is, the design and construction of a comic book page.

Vocabulary

- **Panel**: A panel is a portion of a comic book page that is separated from others. A single panel typically represents a moment in time, a single action, or a setting. The panel is the basic unit of storytelling in a comic book. Panels can contain word balloons, captions, artwork, or any combination of the above. Panels are usually square or rectangular, with a border of some sort to separate them from other panels. As you will see in the pages that follow, however, this is not always the case.

- **Gutter**: The gutter is the space between panels.

- **Page**: A page is made up of panels. Each page in a comic book, when rendered properly, is a piece of art greater than the sum of its parts. A good comic book artist will consider pacing, time, and story flow when composing the page, so that the page conveys the mood and tone of the story appropriately. A page made up of only one panel is called a "splash page." Historically, a splash page was the first page in a comic book and listed that issue's title and creator credits. In modern comics, any page can be a splash page, and the credits and title can similarly appear anywhere in the issue. In some cases, a single panel will be made of *two* pages, stretching across the fold of the comic. This is called a "two-page spread."

- **Word balloon**: Word balloons are the text-filled bubbles that contain dialogue. There are many shapes and forms for word balloons. The average word balloon is an oval, with black text on a white background. Word balloons that seem "fluffy" or cloudlike usually convey a character's thoughts (much like italics in genre fiction). Jagged word balloons can indicate surprise or outrage, etc. In recent years, colors, shading, and other techniques have been applied both to word balloons and the letters within them to get across a diversity of ideas: telepathy, radio broadcasts, the thunderous speech of godlike characters, whispers, etc. Note that most comic books are lettered entirely in uppercase, with emphasis denoted by the use of boldface.

- **Captions**: Captions are boxes containing text. Like word balloons, they are usually subjected to a variety of effects to create different "moods" or concepts. A caption can be any shape, size, or color. While sometimes used to convey dialogue, they are more often used to impart a character's thoughts or as a narrative device.

📖 **Creators (or creative team)**: This term describes the individual(s) who created the comic book in question. You will usually find a *writer, artist, letterer,* and *editor* credited in the comic book. Note that these functions can be filled by one or more people, acting collectively or individually. A comic book may have one writer and multiple artists, for example, or may be the creation of a single person.

📖 **Writer**: The writer, naturally, writes the comic book. This is not, however limited to "writing the words in the balloons," as many newcomers often think. A comic book writer most often works in one of two ways: full script or plot. In full script, the writer describes the action of the comic book page-by-page and panel-by-panel, almost like a movie script. He or she places characters in their environment, writes their dialogue, and in general creates a "word picture" for the artist to follow. In the plot method, the writer writes a looser script, one that describes the action of the story and its key scenes. It is up to the artist to break down this script into pages and panels. The artwork is then given to the writer, who composes the dialogue based on the artist's decisions. It is possible to have multiple writers on a single comic book. Sometimes, one writer will plot the comic, and a second will write the dialogue after the fact. In other cases, many writers may plot a comic book together, with one of them (or another writer) supplying the dialogue.

📖 **Artist**: Comic books usually have three kinds of artists working on them, although, as noted above, these functions can be performed by one or more people in any combination. A *penciler* does the initial work of laying out the page based on the script. He or she creates each panel, places the figures and settings in the panels, etc. The penciled pages are then passed to an *inker*, who uses black ink to render the pencils into fuller, rounder tones. The inker usually adds depth and shadow to the images—a good inker will bring out and enhance the strengths of a penciler's artwork. A *colorist* takes the inked pages and adds color. There are, of course, exceptions to this general workflow: Comics are produced in black and white, with gray tones instead of colors, etc. Some comics are painted in full color, rendering further artists moot. A comic book can have multiple pencilers, inkers, and colorists, or one person can perform any and all of these functions.

📖 **Letterer**: A letterer places word balloons and captions on the finished artwork and fills them with words based on the script. Letterers also often provide the sound effects prevalent in comics, though sometimes the artist will render them.

Section 4: Types of Comic Books

Recall our admonition earlier: The key word in comic book is "book." Although history has unfairly ghettoized comics as "kids' stuff" and "a bunch of superheroes," comic books can be about any topic, told in any style. They run the gamut of storytelling, including:

📖 *Bone*, a delightful, all-ages fantasy

📖 *Superman*, the classic American superhero known the world over

📖 *Maus*, a Pulitzer Prize-winning account of the Holocaust, told in a highly symbolic visual language, in which the Nazis are cats, the Jews mice

📖 *Palestine*, a journalistic depiction of the Middle East

Some terms that you will hear when describing comic books are:

- **Mainstream**: In the comic book industry, this refers to comic books that appeal not to the mass market mainstream but rather to the mainstream *comic book* reader. As a result, the term usually denotes superhero comics and similar fare.

- **Alternative**: Usually used to describe anything that is *not* mainstream.

- **Independent (or "indy")** : Initially used to describe any comic book that was not published by the two major publishers, DC and Marvel. The term has come to encompass a broad range of material.

- **Comix**: A word coined in the 1960s to describe titles that nowadays would be considered alternative. The comix were titles created as a reaction to the juvenilization of comics compelled by Congress in the 1950s, and usually contained adult humor and sexual and political topics.

Section 5: How to Read a Comic Book

While most people have seen a comic book at some point in their lives, reading one is a skill that often fades when not utilized regularly. We have seen many an otherwise intelligent adult balk when faced with the prospect of reading a comic book, simply because the arrangement of the panels or the juxtaposition of text and art is too alien and, thus, intimidating.

In truth, there is no great trick to reading a comic book. In general, two rules prevail: Read from left to right. Read from top to bottom. A well-designed comic book page will lead the reader naturally from one word balloon to the next, one caption to the next, one panel to the next. To be sure, there are ill-designed pages that confuse the novice, but rest assured that such pages confuse veteran readers as well!

Following are examples of comic book pages to help you learn some layout techniques. They also serve to put the terms and concepts learned in this chapter to use. All examples are from the comic book *Quarantine* (© 1992, 1999 Barry Lyga & Rich Bernatovech), written in the plot style.

Figure 2.1.

This page is a modified splash page: A single large panel with a small inset. Following the rules listed before, we would start reading in the upper left-hand corner with the caption "But it is." Note that the first panel is a traditional panel—it represents a moment in time as the character looks at a newspaper.

The second, larger panel, however, works on multiple levels. The character is still looking at the newspaper, but the images above and behind him are representational—they are not physically present with him, but rather are mental images. As you read down the captions along the right-hand side of this panel, notice that two types of captions are used: The captions with white text on black represent a voice speaking to him in his mind, a voice that, according to the captions, shows him images of "others like him"—to wit, the floating faces in the background. This panel is a good example of one of comics' strengths: the ability to compress time and space together into a single visual "moment." The character's despair and horror come through at the same moment that his internal vision is conveyed to the reader. As a result, the reader experiences events at the same time as the character, leading to greater identification with the character.

Figure 2.2.

This page is an example of how comics can convey emotion without words, simply by the use of particular shadings and panels. The lack of words forces the artwork to carry the storytelling burden. As a result, the reader pays more attention to the art. The use of heavy black to border the panels conveys the darkness of the scene, as a woman is murdered. The bottom tier of panels eschews a background, opting for a figure vanishing into darkness. The result is a sense of foreboding.

The panels in that final tier "slim" as they move to the right, creating a sense of movement—the reader feels as though he or she is in motion with the murderer.

Figure 2.3.

This example uses multiple caption styles and nonlinear panel borders to convey multiple meanings. The lack of any border at all for the top panel "opens up" the scene, fitting for a character flying over the New York skyline. The remaining panels, with their fluid borders, recount flashbacks and are therefore as liquid as memory.

The different caption styles serve to alert the reader to changing voices. The rectangular ones are the flying character's thoughts, while the oblong captions are voices from the past that he recalls.

Figure 2.4.

This page can be challenging for the first-time comic book reader. The top tier of panels flows as usual—left to right, top to bottom. But the bottom two-thirds seems to break the rules. It begins at the right ("Max, this whole thing with Mitch's identity . . .") and then flows *left*, moving down the page, then after "Please don't cry," moves right again for the final panel in which the characters hug.

While nontraditional, this layout still works and is not as difficult to follow as the newcomer might think. The arrangement of panels that looks like a lowercase "r" can really only be read in one fashion, when one stops to think about it. Remember that a page should *flow*. The natural movement of the narrative, then, would be to begin on the right and follow the fall of the panels (which mimic the character's descent into despair). Any other reading would disrupt the flow of the panels.

Figure 2.5.

This is a very traditional comic book layout, with a large panel at the beginning, inset with a smaller one. Notice that the smaller panel and the larger one both reflect the same moment in time, from different perspectives—the character's lightning eyes flare as he electrocutes the rat. Again, this is a strength of comic books—the entire moment is delivered to the reader at a single glance, from two points of view.

Figure 2.6.

Another traditional page layout. Notice that the character's demeanor and position in the first and second panels are the same, forming a bridge between the flashback panel and the present. The reverse-text balloon in the fourth panel again symbolizes some "other" form of communication than speech. In panel seven, the choice to list names in their own word balloons as opposed to all at once provides a visual stop after each one, generating the menacing rhythm that otherwise would have to be heard to be understood. And of course the larger typeface used in the last panel indicates anger and outrage that cannot otherwise be communicated in a soundless medium.

Figure 2.7.

Perhaps the most traditional form of comic book page: the nine-panel grid. Notice how this format works almost like a movie scene. Beginning with a shot of the character flying, the point of view cuts to a ground perspective, then "pans" down to the alleyway, then zooms in on the crowned character before pulling back for a final shot.

The floating balloons with smaller type represent crowd "chatter," connected to no person in particular. Their smaller size hints at their relative importance and their lower volume in relation to the main speaker.

The final caption works on two levels: On the one hand, it is a lead-in to the next scene. On the other, it works as ironic juxtaposition, a narrative comment on the state of this particular world, represented by the scene just witnessed.

A Quick Guide to a Comic Book Page

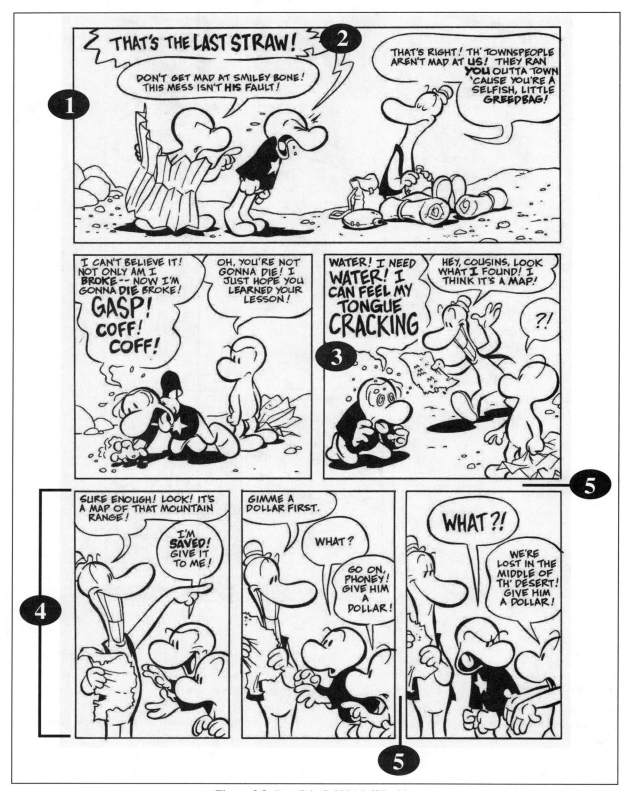

Figure 2.8. *Bone*® is © 2004 Jeff Smith.

1. The box that encloses the action of a scene is the panel border. Panel borders do not always have to be rectangular, nor do they have to exist at all.

2. A word balloon designed to evoke extreme emotion. The jagged edges make the dialogue seem figuratively "sharper" even as the balloon itself is literally sharper.

3. Another word balloon designed to evoke a response. This word balloon's wavering border, with its trembling pointer to the speaking character, gets across the extreme exhaustion that Phoney is feeling.

4. A complete panel.

5. The space between panels (vertically and horizontally) is called a gutter.

3

Graphic Novels for the School Library Media Collection

And now we arrive at the "meat" of the book: the graphic novels themselves. A few caveats before we proceed:

1. No description can substitute for holding a book in your hands and skimming it (preferably reading it in its entirety) for yourself. You know this already, but it bears repeating, *especially* with graphic novels. While we have tried to err on the side of being conservative in our assessments of each title, every community and every school has individual standards. By their very nature, graphic novels present a more visceral experience than a novel or textbook. (See Chapter 5 for further discussion of this topic.) Use our discussion as a guideline, but make your own decisions.

2. There are literally thousands of graphic novels in print, with hundreds more being published every month of the year. A comprehensive overview of all of them in a single resource is almost impossible. The pages that follow contain the merest fraction of available titles. (For a quick look at even more titles, see the appendix.) Be aware that titles come in and out of print regularly, and sometimes even switch publishers.

3. In assembling this list, a deliberate decision was made *not* to discuss certain titles and certain types of titles. You will find a dearth of superhero stories, for example, and a concentration on titles from smaller publishers. Why is this? Because in recent years any number of resources have discussed graphic novels (treating this decades-old medium as a "new" phenomenon in most cases!) tending to focus on a roster of similar titles. At this point, is there an educator who does not know of and understand the benefits of Pulitzer Prize winner *Maus*? And who has not heard of *Superman*, *Spider-Man*, *The X-Men*, *Watchmen*, *Sandman*, etc.? Do not misinterpret the absence of these cherished characters and titles as a denigration of them; in fact, one of your coauthors is a dyed-in-the-wool superhero fanatic. But with so much ink dedicated to these concepts and series so recently, we believe it is more profitable to discuss titles that, in the main, may not have been brought to your attention. (This has an added benefit: When a skeptical colleague or administrator thinks he or she knows all there is to know about graphic novels, you will have ready ammunition at hand!)

What follows are brief descriptions of twenty-five separate titles/series for a variety of age levels. We have provided lesson plans for some as well, which you will find in Chapter 7.

Section 1: Graphic Novels for All Ages

These two titles in particular are great for readers from first grade through graduation . . . and beyond! One you've probably heard of; the other, maybe not. Both are worth your time and consideration.

***Amelia Rules*. Jimmy Gownley.** Harrisburg, PA: Renaissance Press, 2001.

Eisner nominee *Amelia Rules* is a perfect story for parents and children to read, enjoy, and laugh about together. Amelia is an upper-elementary-aged student whose parents are recently divorced. She lives with her mom and her attractive Aunt Tanner (on whom all of Amelia's male friends have crushes). She is a typical kid who enjoys hanging out with her friends, a collection of rambunctious, whimsical kids including Reggie, Pajamaman, and the very-annoying Rhonda. They play games, eat too much food, watch movies, and even form their own superhero club called GASP—the Gathering of Awesome Superpals.

Kids who love *Rugrats* will cheer for *Amelia Rules*, while older readers will recognize a kinder, gentler *Bloom County* humor. Amelia acts like a real kid who has real problems and deals with them through real tears and real humor. With humor, pathos, and honesty, Gownley explores the issues (big and small) that plague kids, from making new friends, to dealing with broken homes, to figuring out how to beat those pesky ninjas in the park. Most important of all, Gownley never talks down to his audience, making this a story for all ages. We recommend it for everyone who can read.

Amelia Rules is projected to be a multivolume series. Volume 1 is currently in print, and volume 2 may be in print by the time you read this.

You can find examples of story and artwork from *Amelia Rules* in Chapter 1 of this book.

Figure 3.1. © 2003 Jimmy Gowley.

See the sample lesson plan in Chapter 7.

Bone. **Jeff Smith.** Columbus, OH: Cartoon Books, 1995.

If there is any title in this book that you've heard of independently, it's probably *Bone*. The mainstream media, the publishing press, and the educational community have been singing the praises of Jeff Smith's *Bone* for close to a decade now, for one reason: It deserves every accolade it gets.

Bone is a mixture of action and adventure, fantasy, and comedy. With so many genres covered, it pleases different types of readers and all ages. The three main characters (cousins Fone Bone, Phoney Bone, and Smiley Bone) are thrown out of their hometown of Boneville. With only a map and their wits, they go exploring for the first time beyond the borders of Boneville into some strange territory and meet some strange characters—human and nonhuman. A gentle romance story line has Fone Bone pining for the beautiful Thorn, with a puppy love feel that will tickle younger and older readers alike.

With a total of nine volumes in the complete series, *Bone* is available in hardback and in softcover. Allyson placed this series in her elementary collection early on and advises media specialists to buy the entire collection; in her experience, once students start with the first volume, they will be back for the rest! She has multiple copies of *Bone* in her media center because one copy of each volume was not enough for her students' needs. She booktalked the books once and has never had to do further promotion—the students talked about it to each other and drove demand from there.

Figure 3.2. *Bone*® is © 2004 Jeff Smith.

Bone has been reviewed in *School Library Journal* (October 2003), *Booklist,* and *Publishers Weekly.* It won Harvey and Eisner Awards in 1993–1995 and 1997–2000, and was a YALSA/ALA Popular Paperback for Young Adults in 2002.

Section 2: Graphic Novels for the Elementary School Collection

***The Collected Alison Dare: Little Miss Adventures.* J. Torres and J. Bone.** Portland, OR: Oni Press, 2002.

Try to imagine a story that combines the adventure of Lara Croft (with none of the sexuality) with the thrills of Indiana Jones (without the bloodshed), and then tosses in a heaping dose of humor and mischief. That's the story of Alison Dare.

This title is for your students who love action and adventure and appreciate the mischievous. Alison Dare is the twelve-year old daughter of an archaeologist mother and a superhero father. With that parentage, her life is far from boring, which is just how Alison likes it—she thrives on adventure and thrills.

But her parents, being parents, would rather she had a calmer life, so they have sent her to a private school, the whimsically named St. Joan of Arc Academy for Girls. Far from keeping her safe, though, school just makes her more likely to get into trouble! With her friends Wendy and Dot, she somehow manages to find herself in the thick of the action, usually in a faraway land.

This is a fabulous book for girls who tend to shy away from the graphic novel format and has the added bonus of a strong female protagonist.

Figure 3.3. *Alison Dare* is ™ and © J. Torres and Jason Bone.

The Collected Alison Dare: Little Miss Adventures has been reviewed on The Diamond Bookshelf.

Figure 3.4. Like every other young girl, when Alison accidentally summons a genie from a lamp,
her first thought is to have her friends teleported to her side . . . no matter what they were doing at the time!
Alison Dare is ™ and © J. Torres and Jason Bone.

Figure 3.5. Notice how the creators make the book educational while still fun, through the device of Alison's bookish friend spouting an elaborate explanation for their predicament. *Alison Dare* is ™ and © J. Torres and Jason Bone.

Li'l Santa. **Thierry Robin and Lewis Trondheim.** New York: NBM Publishing, 2002.

Give this book to your school's reading specialist or special education teacher, and you will have made an instant convert to graphic novels. This is because the format is perfect to teach sequencing, characterization, and story elements . . . all without words!

This wordless graphic novel takes children to the North Pole, where Santa is getting ready for his annual delivery of presents to young children. But this is no ordinary North Pole, and it's no ordinary Christmas! In a wonderful, creative touch, the elves use recycled items such as cans, bottles, and paper to operate the engine of the toy-producing machine, and Santa battles a dragon to deliver the presents.

Students who are reluctant readers will love this book because there is no text to impede their comprehension. This book will shine in comparison to traditional Christmas stories and become a well-loved book in your collection. Best of all, its wordless nature not only lends itself to the whole range of targeted students for graphic novels but also makes it an excellent teaching tool.

Figure 3.6. *Li'l Santa* © 2000 Dupuis & © 2002 NBM.

See the sample lesson plan in Chapter 7, which also includes artwork from this title.

Monkey vs. Robot. **James Kochalka.** Marietta, GA: Top Shelf Productions, 2000.

This is a weird book, perfect for those students who are on the fringe with their quirky sense of humor. We do not mean this as an insult to the book or to the students! But every school has those kids who are particularly gifted or who just have a different way of looking at the world. Sometimes it is hard to find an appropriate book that captures their attention, but *Monkey vs. Robot* fills that void in a wacky, sci-fi fashion. The robot ravishes the forest of its natural resources, threatening the habitat of the monkey. The monkey defends his territory, and all-out war ensures. Is the end actually "The End," or just a new beginning?

This graphic novel is mostly wordless except for some simple sentences spoken by the robot. The illustrations captivate the reader, with not a single detail wasted—every line of the artwork contributes to telling the story. A perfect book for an early, basic economics lesson about human and natural resources, technology and humans, and literary lessons on humans versus nature. (Fine for elementary schools, but most suitable for grade four and up.)

Figure 3.7. *Monkey vs. Robot* © 2000, 2002 James Kochalka. Published by Top Shelf Productions.

See the sample lesson plan in Chapter 7. *Monkey vs. Robot* has been reviewed by *Publishers Weekly* (October 2003).

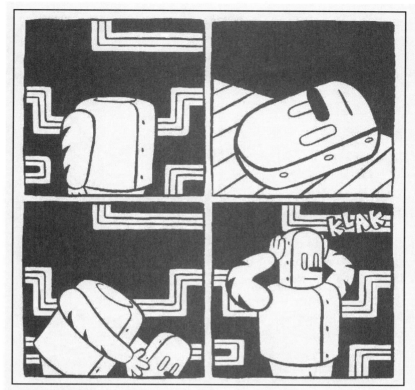

Figure 3.8. In four simple panels, Kolchalka depicts the development of technology from inert force to active antagonist. *Monkey vs. Robot* © 2000, 2002 James Kochalka. Published by Top Shelf Productions.

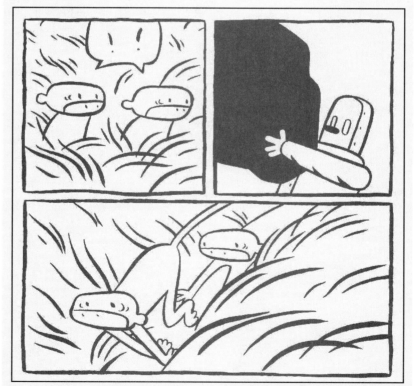

Figure 3.9. The Robot interferes with Nature, upsetting the Monkey's habitat. The visual shorthand conveys a message that any reader can understand. *Monkey vs. Robot* © 2000, 2002 James Kochalka. Published by Top Shelf Productions.

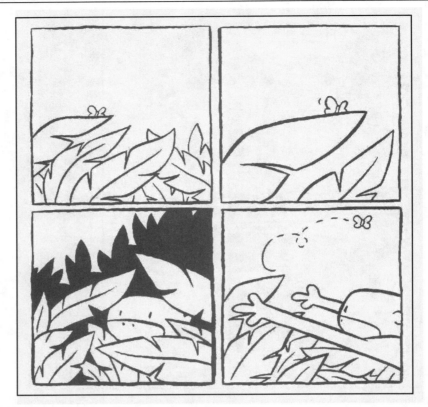

Figure 3.10. The monkey, his environment in ruins, reaches out for the butterfly, as if to take hold of and protect this symbol of his natural, pristine home, which no longer exists.
Monkey vs. Robot © 2000, 2002 James Kochalka. Published by Top Shelf Productions.

Pinky & Stinky. **James Kochalka.** Marietta, GA: Top Shelf Productions, 2002.

Every elementary school media center needs a good animal fiction book, and *Pinky & Stinky* is a wonderful addition to your everybody/easy fiction collection. This is a typical good versus evil story, except in this case the "good" are pigs! Naturally, the students will love to root for the pigs. Pinky and Stinky are two "little cuties" who are the first pig astronauts to go to Pluto. However, they crash into the moon before they make it to Pluto and meet American astronauts stationed there. A battle ensues between the Moon-Men and the American astronauts, and the dear pig astronauts come out as heroes.

This book is a perfect read for the story itself or could be used to start a conversation on racism, space exploration, or capitalism. Suitable for third grade and up, including YA. Very bold, yet simple illustrations.

Figure 3.11. *Pinky & Stinky* © 2002 James Kochalka. Published by Top Shelf Productions.

See the sample lesson plan in Chapter 7.

Figure 3.12. Humor that children can understand, with issues they will relate to.
Pinky & Stinky © 2002 James Kochalka. Published by Top Shelf Productions.

Figure 3.13. After crash-landing on the moon, Stinky wants to forge on while Pinky just gets depressed.
As the story develops, Stinky's fortitude comes through, teaching children a valuable lesson about not quitting.
Pinky & Stinky © 2002 James Kochalka. Published by Top Shelf Productions.

***Scary Godmother.* Jill Thompson.** San Antonio, TX: Sirius Entertainment, Inc., 1999.

***Scary Godmother: The Mystery Date.* Jill Thompson.** San Antonio, TX: Sirius Entertainment, Inc., 1999.

***Scary Godmother: The Boo Flu.* Jill Thompson.** San Antonio, TX: Sirius Entertainment, Inc., 2000.

Allyson has all three of these *Scary Godmother* titles in her collection (there are three more as well), and they never stay on the shelf. Even though the books have a Halloween setting, students fight over them and put them on reserve all year round. Any book that motivates elementary children of both genders to read is a must-have for your collection. These are adorable stories with beautiful painted illustrations for young and old eyes to enjoy.

Scary Godmother is the delightful story of little Hannah Marie and her first Halloween adventure trick-or-treating with the "big kids." When she starts to slow the older kids down, her cousin Jimmy devises a plan to scare her so that she wants to go home early and leave the rest of the evening free for more "big kid" trick-or-treating. They challenge her to put her candy on the basement step for a monster that lives inside a creepy abandoned house. However, once Hannah Marie is inside, she befriends Scary Godmother and other monster friends, who not only manage to save her enjoyment of Halloween but also teach her cousin Jimmy a good lesson about playing tricks on weaker, smaller children.

A great, fun series that teaches a lesson without being preachy. *Scary Godmother* has been reviewed by *School Library Journal* (February 2003).

Sock Monkey: Glass Doorknob. **Tony Millionaire.** Milwaukie, OR: Dark Horse Maverick, 2002.

Sock Monkey and his three friends—Stormy, Inches, and Crow—are amazed by a rainbow created by a glass doorknob. However, as summer's foliage thickens, the doorknob's light is blocked. So the friends search the house for glass and crystal items to help bring the rainbow back. The glass items do not help, but the rainbow returns as fall brings the leaves off the trees.

This book blends the traditional picture book with the graphic novel through the added feature of a continuing comic on the lower left-hand corner of every page, giving it a Jan Brett-like feel. There could be many curricular tie-ins to this book, such as light refraction, prisms, rainbows, and color spectrum, which makes it a perfect choice for those teachers who ask you for "a nice story to introduce rainbows for my science lesson." A great addition to the elementary collection without any language or graphic concerns.

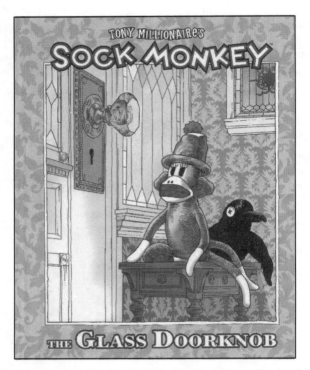

Figure 3.14. *Sock Monkey.* Published by Dark Horse Comics, Inc.

Sundiata: A Legend of Africa. **Will Eisner.** New York: NBM Publishing, 2002.

Most elementary media collections contain every folk tale, fairy tale, and legend under the sun, but you probably don't have anything like the story of *Sundiata*. Even if you do, you'll want to add Eisner's version to your collection, because the layout of this graphic novel dramatically drives home the passion and emotion of the story. Will Eisner is one of the most respected names in graphic novels, having begun his career in the 1940s with his creation, The Spirit. To this day he continues writing and drawing stories, running the gamut from slice-of-life stories to autobiographical fictions to adaptations.

While most folk tales have illustrations that are superior to the story, Eisner's graphic novel re-creation of the African legend of Sundiata does an excellent job of marrying the text and pictures. *Sundiata* is the tale of the evil king Suman Guru's quest to conquer the peaceful land of Mali. When Suman Guru dismisses Sundiata's powers because he was once a sickly child, he discovers the hard way why Sundiata, the adult, is the supreme leader and ruler of Mali. The art and dusty colors of the graphic novel really depict the setting of ancient Africa. The perfect addition to the folk and fairy tale section of any elementary collection, and a suitable addition to a middle school collection for curricular tie-ins to a study on ancient Africa.

Figure 3.15. © 2002 Will Eisner.

See the sample lesson plan in Chapter 7. *Sundiata* has been reviewed in *Publishers Weekly* (November 2002).

Figure 3.16. The dramatic, passionate artwork conveys the depth of the story and character in ways that mere text often cannot. © 2002 Will Eisner.

15

Figure 3.17. Note how Eisner's art provides a sense of place, giving the story context for a modern reader. Students will *see* what it was like to live in ancient Africa, making history come alive for them. © 2002 Will Eisner. Used by permission.

What's Michael? Michael's Favorite Spot. **Makoto Kobayashi.** Milwaukie, OR: Dark Horse Comics, 2002.

Allyson loves *What's Michael?* because the title character in this Japanese series of graphic novels is an adorable, adventurous cat. Each volume in the series is a wonderful collection of short stories about the fun-loving cat, Michael. Since this graphic novel is manga (the Japanese word for comic book), children will be exposed to Japanese names and family life. Children who adore Garfield will enjoy the humor of Michael's adventures with his family, other cats, and even criminals. (Adults will also appreciate its sly humor, such as a funny parody of *The Fugitive* involving a veterinarian.) This book is very easy to read and would be perfect for those students who want to take a thick, heavy book out of the library even though the reading level is way above them. This book is recommended for upper elementary ages.

Concerns: *What's Michael?* does have the occasional "damn it" and "hell" for expressive purposes. These words are not a concern in Japan, but if your area is conservative, this might not be an appropriate book for young elementary children.

Figure 3.18. *What's Michael?* Published by Dark Horse Comics, Inc.

Figure 3.19. An example of the absurd humor in *What's Michael?*: The title feline dons a pair of boxing gloves for a bout. *What's Michael?* Published by Dark Horse Comics, Inc.

Figure 3.20. Even without words, this page conveys action, reaction, and plot development. And without moving, Michael manages to stop a mobster dead in his tracks. *What's Michael?* Published by Dark Horse Comics, Inc.

Figure 3.21. The villain from the previous page meets his match in a collection of cats.
What's Michael? Published by Dark Horse Comics, Inc.

The Wolves in the Walls. **Neil Gaiman and Dave McKean.** New York: HarperCollins, 2003.

This book's type font and illustrations evoke Jon Scieszka; students who like the illustrations of the Stinky Cheese Man will be fans of *The Wolves in the Walls.*

Lucy hears the sound of wolves in the walls, but no one in her family believes her. When the wolves start to come out of the walls, the family flees to the end of the garden to spend the night. Desperate for her pink-pig puppet, Lucy sneaks back inside the house and hides inside the walls. She returns to tell her parents that to live in the house, they too must go inside the walls and scare out the wolves.

The incredible illustrations and layout give this book a picture book feel, but graphic novel panels sprinkled throughout make the experience a unique read. This would be a great read-aloud story for students, but also an appropriate book for students who need visual support to read independently. An excellent story for all ages, and, as an added bonus, author Neil Gaiman is the best-selling author of books for both children (*Coraline*) and adults (*American Gods*), further illustrating the point that graphic novels are a worthwhile addition to your collection.

See the sample lesson plan in Chapter 7. *The Wolves in the Walls* has been reviewed by *Publishers Weekly* (August 2003).

Section 3: Graphic Novels for the Middle School Collection

Note that many middle school titles are also appropriate for high school use.

Castle Waiting. **Linda Medley.** Columbus, OH: Olio Press, 2000.

If your English department studies Renaissance literature and/or British literature, or fairy tales as literature, you need to buy this book, read it, and then have a meeting with those very apprehensive English teachers and sell them this book. Start off by asking, "How would you like to have the most negative, reluctant English students excited by what you are teaching?" If you include *Castle Waiting* in your collection, this will happen.

Ever wonder what happened after "happily ever after?" Now you can find out. Linda Medley's story takes us along on Lady Jain's journey in search of a castle for refuge for herself and her soon-to-be born baby. She meets characters from Mother Goose, the Grimm brothers, and a few new fairy tale creations. The setting of the story, the situations, and the language give this book a very old English/British feel, which is an excellent jumping-off point for classroom discussions about British history and medieval life. Medley includes a vocabulary list for reference. The pictures themselves lend to the humor and fairy tale feel of the story. *Castle Waiting* is a series, so save money in your budget to buy them all—you won't regret it!

Author's Note: *Castle Waiting* was originally published by Olio Press, but as this book was being written, Ms. Medley informed us that publication would be switched to Dark Horse Comics in 2004. By the time this book is in print, the *Castle Waiting* series should be available from Dark Horse.

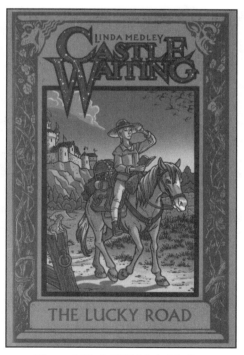

Figure 3.22. © 2003 Linda Medley.

See the sample lesson plans in Chapter 7, designed to cover the whole of *Castle Waiting Volume 1: The Lucky Road*.

Meridian. **Barbara Kesel et al.** Oldsmar, FL: CrossGeneration Comics, 2001.

Science fiction choices at the young adult age tend to exclude girls. The story lines are too extreme and the characters are not appealing from a girl's' point of view. *Meridian*—a science fiction graphic novel for girls—does a wonderful job of embracing girls as readers because the story line is not patronizing or "dumbed-down." The art is amazing, with beautiful painted pictures and gorgeous colors. Readers are drawn to the book based on the cover itself.

Sephie, the main character, is an awkward, tomboy-like teenaged girl who isn't perfect, has problems, and gets into trouble, especially now that her father has died, leaving her in charge of the city of Meridian. The problem, though, is that her uncle has plans to take the city for his own purposes, and Sephie, after all, is young and has much to learn. Aside from living in a world that blends futurism and fantasy, she is your everyday, average teenager and stands out as a reasonable role model, as distinct from the more buxom superheroines who populate the boys' comics.

A super choice for female readers that will have them coming to you for more titles in the *Meridian* series.

Be sure to read the publisher entry on CrossGen in Chapter 6 to learn about the publisher's "Bridges" program, which provides teaching materials for certain titles, including *Meridian.*

Figure 3.23.

Meridian has been reviewed in *School Library Journal* (May 2003).

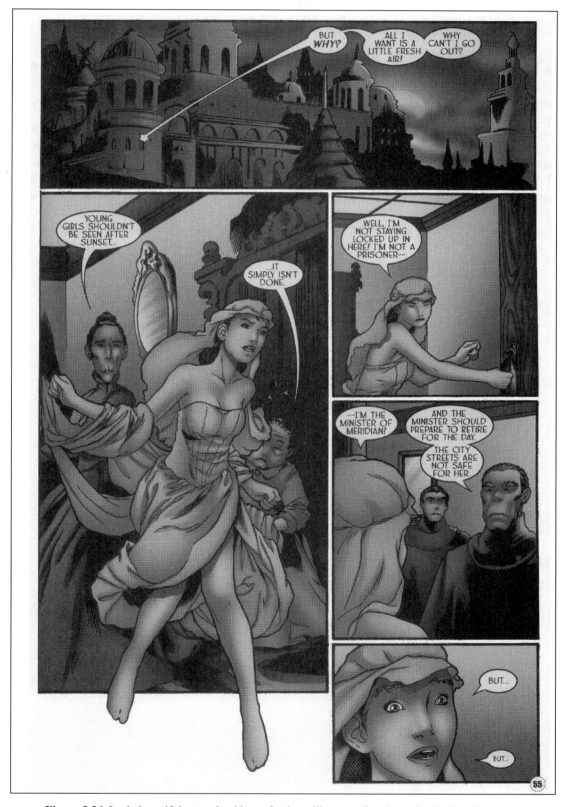

Figure 3.24. Lush, beautiful artwork with a soft edge will engage female readers in *Meridian*'s story. Sephie's natural teenage rebellious streak is about to get her into trouble.

Sweaterweather. **Sara Varon.** Gainesville, FL: Alternative Comics, 2003.

This book is perfect for those students who never read for pleasure and avoid the media center at all costs. Once you put this book in your media center, students will be flocking in to check out books just for fun. In fact, it might even inspire some students to write graphic novels on their own. *Sweaterweather* is eighty-six pages (in partial color) of short comics and other fun things, such as paper dolls and postcards.

Middle schools that have character education programs can study this book for its message of charity, sacrifice, friendship, and integrity. The short comics stories include "Turtle Comic," "Alphabet Sandwiches," and "Winter." "Turtle Comic" is about a turtle and a rabbit on a snowy journey and how each helps the other by dealing with the cold. "Alphabet Sandwiches" employs twenty-six panels, each using a letter of the alphabet, to tell the story of two friends (a boy and his cat) on a shopping trip for ingredients to make a turkey sandwich. Some of the stories are completely wordless; others have dialogue between the two characters and some color. This book is quite endearing for those who want simple, pleasurable stories. If it weren't for one panel showing the popular magazine *Bitch*, this book would be suitable for elementary ages, but some parents may be offended by the magazine title (even though it is an actual publication on newsstands).

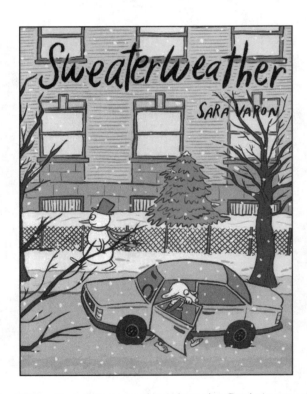

Figure 3.25. © Sara Varon. From *Sweaterweather* (Alternative Comics), www.chickenopolis.com.

Sweaterweather has been reviewed by *The New York Times* (January 11, 2004).

Figures 3.26 and 3.27. © Sara Varon. From *Sweaterweather* (Alternative Comics), www.chickenopolis.com. Wordlessly, Varon crafts complete stories in as little as two pages. These two sequences are both excerpted from larger stories, but notice how Varon is able to convey mood, character, action, and plot development in such a short amount of time and space.

three fingers. **Rich Koslowski.** Marietta, GA: Top Shelf Productions, 2002.

You know those students who dress in black and like the macabre and conspiracy theories? Well, here is a book to reach out to those students and their need for dark stories. *three fingers* parodies Walt Disney's successful cartoon creations and rise to fame, aping the documentary style of shows like *Behind the Music* using cartoon characters. As do all such documentaries, it involves secrets, reversals, and exposés, as well as a conspiracy theory explaining why only those 'toons with three fingers are popular and wealthy.

This is a richly imaginative story and would be a wonderful book to use in starting a graphic novel reading club. You might be surprised at the variety of readers this book will attract.

Figure 3.28. *three fingers* © 2002 Rich Koslowski. Published by Top Shelf Productions.

three fingers has been reviewed by *Publishers Weekly* (July 2002).

Figure 3.29. Older readers (such as your authors!) will recognize this fellow from his silhouette, if not from his accent! But given the sordid secrets he's revealing, it's no wonder he wants to keep his face in the shadows. *three fingers* © 2002 Rich Koslowski. Published by Top Shelf Productions.

Figure 3.30. Rickey Rat drives home the truth behind this dark parody. *three fingers* © 2002 Rich Koslowski. Published by Top Shelf Productions.

Usagi Yojimbo. **Stan Sakai.** Milwaukie, OR: Dark Horse Comics, 1999.

If you want students to learn more about Japanese culture and the legends behind powerful samurais, *and* to enjoy fantastic storytelling, include Sakai's *Usagi Yojimbo* in your collection. Author and illustrator Stan Sakai is well respected and an award-winning creator. Having his books in your media collection is the equivalent of having Russell Freedman, Chris Crutcher, or Laurie Halse Anderson.

Usagi Yojimbo has been a mainstay of the independent comics world for years. Since the protagonist is a sword-wielding rabbit, the book is unfairly pigeonholed as a "funny animal" book. While the characters are animals and the book is often quite funny, nothing could be farther from the truth. As is Art Spiegelman's *Maus*, *Usagi Yojimbo* is filled with real people. They just happen to be *drawn* like animals.

Usagi himself is a lordless samurai, a ronin, wandering in late eighteenth-century Japan, a time of the Shogun's peace, when a strong central lord made samurai such as himself less and less necessary. While some samurai reacted by becoming thieves and bandits, Usagi's path takes him throughout Japan, in search of peace, harmony, and a place to spend the night. Along the way, he becomes embroiled with a fascinating cast of characters, all of whom are also seeking their own way in this strange new world.

Sakai intertwines the history, the code of conduct, and the language of samurai warriors in the story to give it believability and credibility. His research is meticulous, and he annotates each volume with notes that show the historical accuracy of his story, despite the anthropomorphic characters.

This book has everything fans of martial arts movies love: action, mystery, adventure, and drama. However, the best part is that students will be *reading* the story instead of watching it.

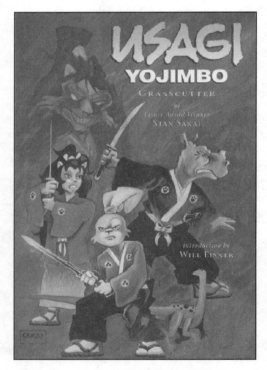

Figure 3.31. *Usagi Yojimbo.* Published by Dark Horse Comics.

Usagi Yojimbo has been reviewed by *Publishers Weekly* (January 2003) and is mentioned in *School Library Journal's* "Building a Strong Collection" (May 2003).

The Yellow Jar, Volume 1. **Patrick Atangan.** New York: NBM Publishing, 2002

The Yellow Jar should be put in middle school and high school collections, for students *and* teachers to appreciate this gem of a book. Beautifully illustrated to emulate the style and colors of old Japanese woodblock prints, this book will work in your collection in many ways, from classes studying Japanese folk tales to art teachers wanting modern examples of Japanese woodblock prints.

Patrick Atangan is amazingly talented at reproducing the style of Japanese woodblock prints, then using them within the context of a graphic novel. *The Yellow Jar* contains two Japanese folk tales about searching for love and honesty. The folk tales chosen are perfect for a literature class discussion on love, but it's the illustrations that will truly move the reader. (Allyson saw original Japanese woodblock prints while in Hagi, Japan, and was amazed by Atangan's fidelity to the original style and the talent this American artist brings to bear on his subject matter.)

Figure 3.32. © 2002 Patrick Atangan. Published by NBM Publishing.

The Yellow Jar has been reviewed by *School Library Journal* (October 2003). See the sample lesson plan in Chapter 7.

Figure 3.33. In a single page, Atangan evokes the setting of old Japan and also establishes character and mood, while proving himself to be a master of Japanese style. The authentic background details and clothing serve as an excellent lesson in history and culture, with many of the accoutrements shown still being used in contemporary Japanese *noh* theater. Note Atangan's use of panels, as the page's primary image is broken up into five panels, each with its own caption, to mimic the passage of time and to establish pacing. © 2002 Patrick Atangan. Published by NBM Publishing.

Section 4: Graphic Novels for the High School Collection

300. **Frank Miller.** Milwaukie, OR: Dark Horse Comics, 1999.

Get this book for your high school collection—you have never had *anything* that will draw boys into your media center like this. This book has been meticulously researched and is based on the true story of Persia's attack on Greece and the 300 members of the Spartan army who sacrificed their lives to defend their country. It is unbelievably rich with action and detail, which probably explains why it won a Harvey Award in the comics industry. Boys who love war stories and action and adventure will love this book and share it with their friends. Students who love Greek myths and/or culture will enjoy every page. Teachers of Greece and Greek history can use this book, for it accurately depicts the Greek hero and the honor and sacrifice of being a soldier. Amazingly rich in detail, art, and facts, *300* is a winner.

Figure 3.34. *300.* Published by Dark Horse Comics.

300 has been reviewed in *Publishers Weekly* (January 2003).

Age of Bronze: A Thousand Ships. **Eric Shanower.** Orange, CA: Image, 2001.

Allyson was enthralled by the work and research that went into this historical depiction of the Trojan War . . . so much so that she wished it had been published when she was taking ancient history in high school—things would have been easier to understand with this book!

Shanower's book could be used as a primer for any high school class dealing with Greek culture and myths. From the pictures to the clothing to the language and geography, *Age of Bronze: A Thousand Ships* does a masterful job of storytelling, right down to the smallest details on a map. There is a plethora of references included in this book, which makes it every educator's dream. There is a seven-page afterword, a four-page name glossary, a genealogical chart on the Achaeans, a genealogical chart on the Trojan Royal family, and a nine-page bibliography. Pair this book with *300* and you will have the start of a wonderful collection of Greek-themed graphic novels.

The first in Shanower's projected series of volumes recounting the Trojan War, *Age of Bronze: A Thousand Ships* is a winner of the Eisner Award and also contains some risqué (historically accurate) subject matter, so more conservative schools will want to preview it before adding it to the collection.

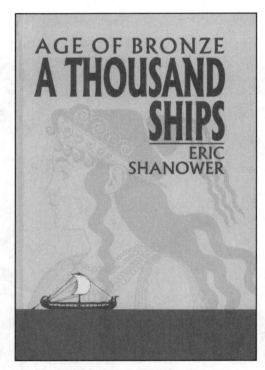

Figure 3.35. ™ & © 2004 Eric Shanower.

See the sample unit plan in Chapter 7.

Concrete: Killer Smile. **Paul Chadwick.** Milwaukie, OR: Dark Horse Comics, 1995.

What should have been an ordinary trip to the gas station ends up a nightmare for Larry Munro: He is kidnapped by two brutal and sadistic murderers on the run. Fortunately for Larry, he happens to be the personal assistant to Concrete, a former speechwriter who has been imprisoned in a massive, powerful concrete body. But this isn't the story of your typical superhero, and Concrete can't just fly in to save the day. This is Larry's story, as he struggles to survive, attempting to outwit his kidnappers and live to tell the tale. Larry's faith in his friend, Concrete, is always in the back of his mind as he is held hostage, and his friendship becomes the touchstone that keeps him sane during his ordeal.

Unlike so many stories in this vein, Chadwick also presents a series of flashbacks to the childhoods of the *kidnappers*, showing why they are so ready to inflict pain and disregard the feelings of others. A dark, starkly told story, *Killer Smile* should be in high school collections so that students can understand the motivations of one human and how the decisions one person makes can intersect with other lives. Also great for psychology and sociology classes, to show how childhood and class can influence the decisions we make as adults.

There are other volumes in the *Concrete* series, all of which deal with Concrete and his circle of friends as he tries to live as normal a life as possible within the confines of the monstrous body he's been given.

Figure 3.36. *Concrete.* Published by Dark Horse Comics.

Figure 3.37. The reader's introduction to Concrete. Note the details Chadwick employs to get across Concrete's size, power, and unique problems: the chair made of cinder blocks (crumbling where he's strummed with his fingers) and the open space of his room. Also, notice how Concrete is introduced to the reader: sitting at home in his chair, relaxing, almost shoved into the background. This is clearly a *very* different kind of "superhero." *Concrete*. Published by Dark Horse Comics.

Figure 3.38. Concrete's friend is abducted at gunpoint in a scene filled with tension and fear. *Concrete.* Published by Dark Horse Comics.

Figure 3.39. While Larry lives as a hostage, in fear for his life, Concrete is essentially powerless, unaware of his friend's plight and left with the option of simply waiting outside for Larry to arrive. An excellent way to talk to students about the nature of bravery and heroism, and how power does not necessarily give one the ability to fix problems. *Concrete.* Published by Dark Horse Comics.

Crayon ShinChan. **Yoshito Usui.** Fremont, CA: ComicsOne, 2002.

This book is a necessity for your high school collection because you will have faculty members who are parents, *and* students who love manga, fighting over this hilarious book! Word of mouth will spread when you put this book in your collection—you will probably need to buy multiple copies because *everyone* will want to read it.

The *Crayon ShinChan* series is a fun read; it would be suitable for any class that is studying Japan and wants a modern insight into the culture, complete with an honest, accurate portrayal of Japanese humor about bodily functions and nudity. It chronicles the life of a five-year-old boy who loves getting into trouble by being offensive, embarrassing, and tricky. ShinChan takes great pleasure in getting into trouble, all the while pretending to be totally innocent. While the specifics are Japanese, the themes and hilarity are universal. Allyson's time in Japan convinced her that this book could serve as an excellent primer for Japan's cultural acceptance of nudity, bath customs, and humor.

Figure 3.40. © 1992 Yoshito Usui.

Crayon ShinChan has been reviewed on The Diamond Bookshelf. See the sample lesson plan in Chapter 7.

Figure 3.41. Little ShinChan goes overboard with his adherence to social mores and customs, forcing the elevator operator to look her passengers in the eye and asking some very inappropriate questions. © 1992 Yoshito Usui.

Figure 3.42. In the tradition of children everywhere, ShinChan drives his mother crazy. © 1992 Yoshito Usui.

Figure 3.43. ShinChan tries to train his new dog but isn't quite clear on exactly what the dog can do, much to Mom's chagrin and annoyance. © 1992 Yoshito Usui.

Moby Dick. **Will Eisner.** New York, NBM Publishing, 1998.

Students who have to read *Moby Dick* for American literature but are intimidated by the text will be grateful for Will Eisner's *Moby Dick.* Eisner does a fantastic job of staying true to the story and plot line, but it's the pictures that capture the passion in the search for the big whale. Allyson admits to not being a fan of *Moby Dick* in high school—the density of Melville's narrative obscured the visceral reasons for risking so much to kill the whale. However, with Eisner's expressive artwork complementing the story line, she was much better equipped to appreciate the "man versus nature" conflict and the driving need to conquer.

High school media specialists who purchase this book should march right up to the special education department and show it to them—they will be thrilled to give their students an opportunity to read a classic that fully supports the visually dependent learner.

Figure 3.44. © 1998 Will Eisner.

See the sample lesson plan in Chapter 7. *Moby Dick* has been reviewed by *Publishers Weekly* (January 2003).

Figure 3.45. For those students who can't picture the hunt for the white whale, Eisner's adaptation provides images to convey the story, complete with the ruin and quiet of the famous finale. © 1998 Will Eisner.

Oh My Goddess! Wrong Number. **Kosuke Fujishima.** Milwaukie, OR: Dark Horse Comics, 2002.

Students who love fantasy and manga will enjoy this story of college student Keiichi Morisato and his adventures with the goddess Belldandy, whom he accidentally summons one night when he calls the goddess technical support line instead of his roommate. Keiichi is known as a geek. He never gets the girls; he isn't seen as handsome or talented; and when Belldandy asks him to make one wish, he jokingly asks for her to stay with him forever. "Be careful what you wish for" never applied more—his wish comes true! Now in addition to college, he has to deal with life with a very powerful and beautiful goddess. Belldandy just doesn't "fit in" on the mortal plane, casting spells at the wrong time and generally making Keiichi's life more chaotic than usual. Girls will love this book because the source of power is a woman; Belldandy controls every situation with her magic. Teenagers will relate to Keiichi and Belldandy's inability to blend in and their everlasting relationship troubles. The romantic overtones make this a truly magical comedy.

Figure 3.46. *Oh My Goddess!* Published by Dark Horse Comics.

Oh My Goddess! was selected by ALA for its Quick Picks for Reluctant Young Adult Readers.

Figure 3.47. Introducing the goddess Belldandy. Keiichi is about to make a decision that will change the rest of his life. *Oh My Goddess!* Published by Dark Horse Comics.

Ranma ½. **Rumiko Takahashi.** San Francisco: Viz Communications, 2002.

Allyson's favorite manga is *Ranma ½*, a wonderful choice to include in your collection. Tendo owns a martial arts school and has three daughters, all whom are proficient in martial arts themselves. The only problem is that Tendo would like one of the girls to marry so that his training center will be secure and stay in the family. Tendo arranges for his friend's son, Ranma Saotome, to come from China for an extended visit in hopes of arranging a marriage with one of his daughters.

Ranma is a bit uncultured and rude but quick-witted. He is very skillful in martial arts, which usually lands him in trouble when one of the daughters challenges him to a duel. But all is not as it seems—when Ranma comes into contact with cold water things get weird. Due to an ancient curse, he turns into a beautiful young woman! (Hot water reverses the effect.)

Part teen romance, part sex farce, and all heart, *Ranma ½* is one of the most popular manga titles in Japan, spanning more than twenty separate volumes as Ranma struggles with his own identity and an ever-growing (and ever-more bizarre!) cast of friends, foes, and just plain weirdos.

Beyond its action-packed, hilarious story, we recommend the book for its insight into Japanese culture, from the architecture, to school uniforms, to the food, to the ubiquitous bathing rituals. A wonderful addition to any middle school or high school humorous fiction collection. (**Note:** Nudity is sometimes employed for comedic effect, but never for salacious purposes.)

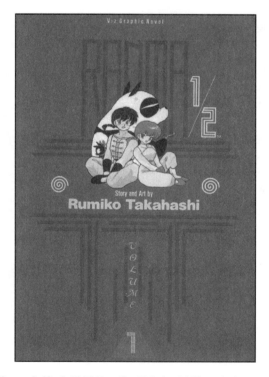

Figure 3.48. © 1988 Rumiko Takahashi/Shogakukan, Inc.

Summer of Love. **Debbie Drechsler.** Montreal: Drawn & Quarterly, 2002.

Illustrated in a bizarre red and green scheme that serves to highlight the sense of displacement the characters feel, *Summer of Love* packs quite a story about growing up, sibling rivalry, first loves, and relationships. Girls who enjoy romantic comedies will love this book and share it with their friends. This is "the book" that will be talked about, put on reserve, and basically will never have to be shelved because it will never stay there.

Seventeen magazine liked the book, and while we admit that *Seventeen* is not in the same league as *SLJ,* they *do* know what teenagers enjoy. So put a copy out with a big sign that says "As seen in *Seventeen*" and you will become a hero.

Figure 3.49. © 2004 Debbie Drechsler.

Summer of Love has been reviewed in *Publishers Weekly* (October 2002).

4

Testimonials

Yes, it can be done! You can incorporate graphic novels into your collection. By now, you understand the content, importance, and utility of graphic novels. Before we move on to discuss some resources and support mechanisms for you, it would be instructive to consider the advice and experience of those who have already taken the plunge and incorporated graphic novels into their collections. We spoke to a dozen media specialists and librarians, sampling for diversity, including elementary, middle, and high schools, from areas as varied as Brooklyn, New York, and rural Carroll County, Maryland.

The topic was graphic novels in school libraries, of course, but the questions pertained particularly to those issues that are typically of highest concern to those who are introducing a new "product" to their students: Why did you decide to use graphic novels? How did you start? Did you meet resistance from parents or administrators? How did the students react? How do you catalog and shelve graphic novels? And so on.

Our survey respondents were both men and women, teaching grades from kindergarten through twelfth. One was a public librarian, included in the group to give additional perspective. Another was a former media specialist who is now a classroom teacher using graphic novels in her classroom library. While their selections and their rationales for using graphic novels vary, there are some very important common elements to each, the most notable of which is this: No one surveyed began using graphic novels any sooner than 1998. Most, in fact, had only been using them in a collection for a year or two at the time we contacted them. All of them, however, noticed immediate and dramatic results, even in so short a time period.

One last point before we move on: We have met many media specialists who have told us, in effect, "I know that I should be using graphic novels, but I just don't like them." To which we respond: "Whoever said you *have* to like them?"

Do you like every book in your collection today? Do you like every Web site available on your computers? Of course not. In fact, some of the respondents of our survey are ambivalent about graphic novels: "Frankly, I don't like the [medium]," says Esther Lewenstein, a middle school media specialist from Brooklyn. "To be honest, I have not read [a graphic novel] all the way through," admits Patricia Valas, another middle school media specialist, from New Windsor, Maryland.

As you will see throughout this chapter, however, both have put aside their personal feelings toward graphic novels, seeing them as important tools for the benefit of the students.

Section 1: Why Graphic Novels?

The question "Why graphic novels?" was addressed in an earlier chapter, but from a research and scientific perspective. We now ask why—in practical, real-world terms—specific media specialists chose to incorporate graphic novels into their collections.

Some made their decisions based on the same factors that influence so many decisions: "Students' requests," said sixth grade teacher (and former school librarian) Shannon Resh of York County, Pennsylvania. "The kids love them!" agreed elementary school media specialist Karen Boggs of Finksburg, Maryland. Don't be so quick to dismiss such superficially simplistic answers. As most media specialists know, the first crucial obstacle to breeding a love of the written word in students is getting their attention and making them *want* to be in the library in the first place. Giving students what they want—as long as it is educational and useful in the long run—is a perfectly acceptable and valid way to accomplish this goal. Especially when it works. "It's hard to say, because the collection is new," said Lewenstein, whose collection of graphic novels began in January 2003. "But the preliminary interest shows that they're reading."

Some finally "caved" because of the weight of anecdotal evidence and professional respect accorded graphic novels. Like you, they heard about graphic novels from colleagues, read about them in journals, and saw them mentioned in a variety of contexts. "[I adopted graphic novels due to] an article I read about a study which discussed the benefits of using comic books in the classroom," said Beth McKay (a media specialist at Kingsview Middle School in Germantown, Maryland). "The study noted that comic books had a higher level of vocabulary and students would see lots of new words—more so than in some novels."

By far, however, the most-cited reason for incorporating graphic novels into a school media collection came down to two words: reluctant readers. "I started using graphic novels for two reasons," said high school media specialist Penny Foster (Century High School in Westminster, Maryland). "One, to support the art classes. Also, to support those students with lower reading ability as well as those with little interest in reading." "[My] students have low reading levels, and needed something to inspire them to read. There are a lot of reluctant readers on my campus" added Sharon Gonzalez (Connell Middle School, San Antonio, Texas). From rural Maryland to inner city San Antonio, the reasons are the same.

All well and good to *say* such things and to believe them, but does actual day-to-day experience bear them out? Yes. We specifically asked each media specialist how the mere presence of graphic novels in a collection affected recreational reading attitudes. Bearing in mind that reading attitudes differ between boys and girls, we also asked if they had noticed distinct reactions between boys and girls. In general, responses indicate that (in line with the theories proposed in Chapter 1) boys particularly take to graphic novels: "Right now the collection is particularly popular with middle school boys," a high school librarian from Virginia (who wished not to be identified) told us. "It is mainly the boys who check them out," Gonzalez agreed, while Boggs noted that "everyone seems to love the *Captain Underpants* series, but I would say the boys are more excited than the girls." (See "Boys and Girls and Graphic Novels.")

Boys and Girls and Graphic Novels

Here are some more comments the media specialists in our survey focus group offered when asked about the reactions of students to the inclusion of graphic novels in their collections:

- "I usually field a lot of questions about our anime books (books with anime as the topic, like Gilles Poitras' books) and drawing books as well. At least half of the students checking out graphic novels usually check out other fiction novels at the same time. Girls are reading the graphic novels, and I hope to attract more by adding *shojo* titles like *Kare Kano*."—S. S., high school, Virginia

- "The graphic novel audience (which includes girls and boys) makes more frequent trips to the media center."—Patricia Valas, middle school, Maryland

- "It has affected recreational reading habits in boys somewhat."—Jan Nies, elementary school, Maryland

- "Mainly boys, and some of the girls who are not strong readers really love them. Even when they are just hanging out in the Teen Room they take one and sit and read it."—Ann Marie Naples, public library, Connecticut

- "The boys scramble to get them, come in with a friend who is returning one so they can be the next person to get the book. They are making use of our system of holds. They go beyond the class requirement of checking out a book, and come in before school and during lunch to get them!"—Sharon Gonzalez, middle school, Texas

- "The boys *loved* the collection and would read anything new to the rack. The girls were more selective, and waited for specific titles. The overwhelming use was from the boys, however."—Shannon Resh, grade six, Pennsylvania

The proof of the pudding, however, is in the eating. Or, in this case, in the circulation. Circ rates tell the tale as to the *true* popularity of a book, as anyone who has ever tried to keep a copy of *Harry Potter* on the shelf can tell you! In Chapter 5, two comic book store owners discuss some interesting circulation numbers they've encountered, but our survey group had its own experience in that area.

In general, graphic novels circulated *at least* as much as other books. No one in the group said that they circulated less. On the contrary, most reported that graphic novels circulate *more often* than other books: "No doubt about it," said Lewenstein. Our group acknowledged that graphic novels circulate on a par with popular fiction titles like *Harry Potter, Holes,* the *Sevens* series, or *Lemony Snicket,* forcing at least one media specialist to put shorter due dates on graphic novels! Boggs pointed out that the only books in her collection with higher circulation are the *Guinness Book of World Records* and *The Complete Dog Book for Kids,* both nonfiction books.

When asked how graphic novels meet the needs of reluctant readers in particular, our focus group was enthusiastic about the results, pointing out that graphic novels make an "Easier transition from not reading novels to [works such as the] fantasy genre," and that "reluctant readers are more likely to choose them."

"The kids see the pictures and think they're not reading. But we fooled them, because they are," pointed out Lewenstein, striking an important chord in the use of graphic novels. While some parents may decry graphic novels as "not really reading a book," the information presented in Chapter 1 gives the lie to this notion. McKay pointed out that she has "never had a reluctant reader turn down a comic book—I guess that's why I use them—to get to those readers." Boggs mentioned that, in her experience, children who normally do not check books out *will* check out graphic novels. The graphic novels work so well that even skeptics are convinced: "I feel that while graphic novels are not in the same league as a good [prose] book, they serve a group of patrons who might not read at all," admitted Anne Marie Naples, the teen librarian for the New Britain public library in Connecticut. (Although Ms. Naples represents a public library, her experiences can be of value to the media specialist who is interested in adding graphic novels to a collection. In fact, media specialists may want to consider the presence of graphic novels in their local public libraries when they plan their additions to the school media collection.)

Why are graphic novels so successful with reluctant readers? Here are some concrete reasons derived from the experiences of our focus group:

- "They [graphic novels] don't look as intimidating as a textbook. Also, they often have familiar characters from film or TV, so students already know something about the story and have a connection to the characters."

- "High interest, short text passages, visual clues."

- "Short text, lots of pictures, a book they can actually understand and finish! Fast action, little description—mostly conversation."

- "The graphic novels are far less intimidating for the reluctant reader. Instead of pages covered with words, they can read pictures and words. For those with decoding disabilities, the pictures provide an additional method to identify meaning."

The ultimate support comes from middle school media specialist McKay, who said that graphic novels have "helped some of my lower level boys to realize that reading for pleasure is one of the greatest things they can do." Most media specialists will confess that getting reluctant readers to read *at all* is one of their most difficult tasks, and that getting them to read simply for pleasure is nearly impossible. Graphic novels can point the way and help you to accomplish this difficult yet crucial goal.

All in all, Lewenstein summarized the argument best: "There are many reluctant readers in the school I work in. I knew that by incorporating these titles, more students would come and use the library and *I was right*" (emphasis added).

Section 2: Practical Matters

Once you know that graphic novels work and have a reasonable expectation of what to expect from them, you will have a range of practical questions. This book exists mainly to answer those questions, but we thought it might be instructive to see how others in your position have dealt with them as well. So let us briefly discuss such quotidian issues as whether to buy softcover or hardcover graphic novels, and how to decide which graphic novels to buy in the first place.

Getting Started

There is no hard-and-fast set of rules that dictate which titles to include in a collection, or which titles to use when starting a collection. Nor is there any rule regarding how many graphic novels you need to shelve to consider them a viable, working part of your collection. In our survey, school libraries shelved from as few as half a dozen titles up to more than a hundred. Obviously, the more graphic novels you incorporate, the more positive impact they'll have, and the greater your chances of using graphic novels that appeal to your students. Ultimately, this is the most important criterion: your individual school environment. While we are of the opinion that a smattering of graphic novels will not do much good, some of the respondents to our survey have seen pleasant results with just a few titles. For example, Keith Taylor (an elementary school librarian in Eldersburg, Maryland) carries only the *Captain Underpants* series in his graphic novel collection but is impressed enough with the results that he plans to expand: "If the students are reading (eyes on print) then this is a positive thing," he says.

Contrast this with Virginia's "S. S.," who had to fight to get graphic novels into the collection, bucking the system to the point that S. S. has requested we not use his or her name or school district. Yet now S. S. has dozens of titles on the shelves, including complete collections of many series with multiple volumes!

How many graphic novels you incorporate initially will depend on a variety of factors: your level of funding, the cooperation of administrators, school district requirements, and more. Likewise, the specific titles and series you choose for your collection will be unique to your situation: What is the grade level in your school? What kind(s) of reader(s) are you trying to reach? Are you interested in titles for recreational reading, or are you trying to tie into the curriculum? For that matter, do you *have* to tie into the curriculum?

In Chapter 5 we introduce you to two gentlemen who have some ideas on these important initial choices, and in Chapter 6 you'll see a wealth of resources to help make them happen. But for now, realize that no two school library collections are alike . . . nor should they be. Our focus group varied wildly in terms of numbers of titles, and also in terms of which titles they used, even when grade levels were similar or identical. One of the beauties of graphic novels is that the selection is so vast that you have the luxury (and the task!) of customizing your collection to fit your tastes, and the tastes of your students, colleagues, and community.

Cataloging

How do you catalog graphic novels? Given their relatively new status in libraries and schools, there are no hard-and-fast standards as of this writing. Some book jobbers and distributors will offer their own cataloging information, and some won't. Some schools insist on doing their own cataloging. Most media specialists tend to make use of one of the following systems:

   741.5: Cataloging all graphic novels under a single Dewey number makes them easy to find and track. Unfortunately, this is not necessarily the most accurate system (not *all* graphic novels should, in fact, be cataloged as 741.5, and some would benefit more from being shelved with different subject matter).

📖 Modified 741.5: This allows the graphic novels to be shelved in a central location, but also singles them out as separate from the rest of the Dewey classification. Lewenstein receives her materials pre-cataloged as 741.5, but then adds "GN" to the call number and places them in a separate section. S. S. uses a similar system: "We have centralized processing, so I don't have a choice about how the books are cataloged. When we get them, I apply a 'Graphic Novels' spine label (available from Demco). The books themselves are kept in the fiction area of the library in a two-shelf bookcase."

📖 Separate section: Some create a special section of the collection for graphic novels, for a variety of reasons: As he expands his collection, Taylor plans "to catalog them like the rest of my collection. I plan to make a category for graphic novels so that I can track their circulation." Foster follows suit: "For cataloging, we put them in GRA so that we can put them in a separate section and highlight them."

📖 Fiction: Many media specialists simply categorize graphic novels as fiction and treat them accordingly. This is a fine solution so long as one recalls that not *all* graphic novels are fiction. Some are autobiography, some are history, some are science, etc. One other concern about placing graphic novels in fiction is their extraordinary popularity, as Gonzalez points out: "I would love to just place them by author in the fiction section, but it would be more difficult for the students to find them, and for me to remember where they are—they would be constantly asking me."

Hardcover or Softcover?

As you will see in Chapter 5, the issue of graphic novels' durability is no longer a real point of contention. Many newcomers to the format, though, tend to shy away from softcover editions, as experience bears out that softcover editions of *any* type (whether graphic novels or prose texts) are weaker than hardcovers. In the current graphic novel publishing climate, there is not always an option of choosing one over the other, however. While some series and titles are available in a variety of formats, the overwhelming majority are available as softcover only.

Should this be an area of concern? In Chapter 5 you'll learn about the durability of graphic novels, and in Chapter 6 you'll see how to increase the shelf life of a softcover title, but for the most part, softcover or hardcover is not an issue that bothered our focus group. While one admitted that buying softcover was "probably a mistake," she gave no indication that she would stop doing so—clearly the benefits of the graphic novels outweighed any disadvantages, real or perceived, of the format. Of the others, most dismissed the issue entirely, expressing no preference for one or the other. Gonzalez's attitude is representative: "The format does not attract or turn off the kids, so it doesn't matter to them. Try for hardbound copies, but don't be put off by the paperbacks. They are holding up."

Sources: Where to Get Graphic Novels

Chapter 6 contains numerous suggestions about where to purchase graphic novels, but bear in mind that no one source is the right one. Depending on your individual circumstances, a solution or source that works for one media specialist may not work for another. In our survey, we discovered school librarians who use traditional book jobbers (such as Follett, BWI, and Brodart), those who use local comic book specialty stores (see the next chapter), and even one who haunts flea markets for titles! Depending on the standards and requirements of your school and school district, you may or may not be able to avail yourself of the many sources for graphic novels. Rest assured, though, that if one source seems closed to you, there is at least one other that will work.

Collection Development

If you're a newcomer to the world of graphic novels, two questions that are most likely uppermost in your mind are, "How do I afford this?" and "Which ones do I buy?" In Chapter 3 we discuss a variety of titles for your consideration, and our appendix contains 100 more. Furthermore, Chapter 6 lists a wealth of resources for reviews and selections. But for now we'd like to illustrate how some of your peers have dealt with these questions.

For the most part, media specialists tend to purchase graphic novels with their regular school allotment, often supplemented by special grants or book fair profits. As to choosing which titles to incorporate, the best, most succinct advice we've encountered comes from S. S.: "I have four factors: story, art (both good), age appropriateness (keeping in mind that our collection is heavily used by middle school students), and appeal. Although that doesn't stop me from adding things (like *Barefoot Gen*) which are not going to be wildly popular but are nevertheless very good." In short, look for quality and age-appropriateness, as well as subjects that will intrigue your students.

To help you make those judgments, many of the resources in Chapter 6 come into play, such as the well-regarded No Flying, No Tights Web site (www.noflyingnotights.com), *Booklist*, *Library Journal*, *School Library Journal*, *VOYA*, books on the topic (such as the one you're reading right now!), and more. S. S. cautions that some resources, such as No Flying, No Tights and the Diamond Bookshelf, may not be considered "accepted professional resources" by all supervisors. Remember your area's requirements when making your selections.

One resource that media specialists tend to fall back on when making choices is student interest. This seemingly obvious choice may sometimes be overlooked, but since you're trying to stimulate the students' reading, doesn't it make sense to give them what they want? (Of course, when you're making curricular connections with graphic novels, you'll need to apply those criteria, but for recreational reading purposes, don't forget to take into account the opinions of the ones doing the reading.)

Penny Foster points out one method that works well for her (and for others, based on our survey): "I used many media journals and read reviews on most of them. I took the lists and definitely got those mentioned on multiple lists." As a result, she has multiple reviews of each item and can be more assured that the book in question truly is worthy, since it appears multiple times.

Foster also points out another useful tool for librarians looking to incorporate graphic novels: "Our art teacher was a great resource." Do not underestimate the utility of your art teacher. You will find an ally in many art teachers, who usually appreciate the skill that goes into creating a graphic novel. Furthermore, art teachers will understand that your graphic novel collection can aid their instruction as well by sparking an interest in art among students. In the best of all possible worlds, your collection will end up encouraging not only reading but also drawing.

Finally, many of those we surveyed sang the praises of the local comic book specialty store, not only as a place to buy graphic novels but also as a place to learn about them. You will get an in-depth look at the comic book store in Chapter 5.

Section 3: Using Graphic Novels with the Help of (or in Spite of!) Others

You now have a better idea of why to use graphic novels, as well as some insight into how to choose and use them. But as we all know, there are often issues beyond the actual efficiency and efficacy of a title on the shelf. Are administrators going to support your decision to use graphic novels? Will parents complain? Will teachers think you've lost your mind?

We can answer the last question at least: probably not. With comic books getting more and more media attention lately (and with much of it being positive), graphic novels are hardly taboo these days. As for the other questions, answering them and deflecting potential criticism and problems is a large part of this book's mission.

Remember that due to their visual nature, graphic novels provide a more visceral, immediate experience. As a result, content that might be considered acceptable in prose may be seen as controversial or too intense when presented in pictures. In short, the sentence, "John shot Bill," is perfectly acceptable in a murder mystery novel that students of a particular age might read, but the same event—when presented as a picture of John shooting Bill, Bill collapsing in pain, his face in anguish—might be seen by some as entirely different. If necessary, be prepared to show how the content of your graphic novels is equal to the content of your prose books.

Resistance

We asked our survey group an obvious question: Did you encounter resistance to graphic novels from teachers, parents, or administrators? Knowing that comic books have historically been looked down upon in education (an attitude that still lingers in some quarters), we were prepared for a bevy of horror stories. Much to our delight, however, the answers were almost universally "no."

"I asked permission and support from administration and the reading supervisor prior to building the collection," said Resh, pointing out one way to defuse potential problems from the get-go. This is, of course, a good policy for *any* new initiative. On the opposite side of the spectrum, sometimes it's best to forge ahead—Gonzalez was "not sure if [my] administrators even know about [my graphic novels]," but went on to say that, far from being appalled at graphic novels, "the teachers are thrilled with them!"

Of course, you may run into problems, as Nies did with the *Captain Underpants* series: "Some teachers do not like *Captain Underpants* due to content and misspelled words." Boggs has had "a few adults, including a cafeteria worker at my school, say that they don't like them, but I've had more adults say how funny they are and how much their kids love them." In neither case, though, did any serious consequences arise. No one called for the expulsion of the titles from the collection, and support continued for the media specialist.

In what could be described as a "worst-case" scenario among those surveyed, "S. S." actually had to work around an obstinate head librarian who was not sanguine about the prospect of graphic novels. "That is the reason my initial order was so limited," S. S. told us. "When I wanted to add *Pedro and Me* (which I had reviewed for the county), she refused, even though I had numerous positive reviews besides my own to support the book's inclusion in the collection." S. S. persevered and eventually carried the day. "I haven't (yet, fingers crossed) had any protests from parents, teachers, or other administrators, and the other library staff members (two more assistant librarians and two aides) are supportive of the books. I mostly overcame resistance by being patient. . . . The students are very enthusiastic about the books, and it's hard to ignore the circ numbers. Also, I take every opportunity I can to let the head librarian know that there are teachers who appreciate the collection, or that a student who couldn't find a graphic novel he wanted walked away happy with a 'real' book."

That last comment may be the most telling: As media specialists, it is important to remind colleagues and administrators of the importance of the collection to the school. Likewise, pointing out the success of your graphic novel initiative reminds those who may be resistant that your instincts and judgment were right. While we are not advocating an "ends justify the means" attitude, it is hard to argue with outright success! (And specific to S. S.'s situation: While S. S. met with initial resistance from the head librarian, that same person later came around and asked S. S. to present a workshop on graphic novels for other librarians in that school system!)

The most important thing we learned in talking about resistance to graphic novels, though, is this: In not a single situation that we examined was a media specialist expressly forbidden from incorporating graphic novels. Even in S. S.'s case, the head librarian was merely reluctant to add graphic novels and made it difficult, but at no point banned them. Armed with information, reviews, and patience, you *will* succeed.

Reactions

Once the graphic novels are safely cataloged and shelved, what sort of reaction should you expect from students, teachers, parents, and the community? Will teachers want to use them in lessons?

We've already discussed student reactions in some detail, both in this chapter and in previous chapters. In short, you can expect a terrific response, along with high circulation figures. Lewenstein told us, "The students love the graphic novels. In just 5 months, the books were falling apart from use. And unlike some books, these books came back, because the kids wanted to read more!" McKay's students (mostly her boys) "love to read the comic books. Some run to the bookshelf so they can get to them first." Isn't that the sort of enthusiasm you want from your students? And isn't that a great way to defuse any potential complaints? (When was the last time students—*boys* in particular—ran for a book?) S. S., who had to fight for graphic novels, told us that "The books are so popular with students that we have had to limit them to taking only two at a time, so that a few students don't wipe out the whole collection at once."

We can expect that children would be excited by graphic novels, but what about the adults you need to contend with? Especially when teachers are interested in graphic novels, you gain important allies in maintaining and improving your graphic novel collection, and these days, in the experience of Shannon Resh, "teachers realize comics are much more that 'CRASH! POW! BANG!' and that they are much more substantial than first realized." S. S. pointed out that "ESOL and special education teachers have been excited about the books," and was asked by a teacher to booktalk graphic novels for her class. Valas was happy to find that a fellow teacher had booktalked them as well.

"The teachers are very pleased," said Gonzalez "The students are actually reading them, and following the plot lines, and they are inspired to read them to the end. They fit into all of the objectives of requiring students to read. Teachers can require character studies, summaries, vocabulary lists, etc. as easily from graphic novels as from using the traditional chapter book."

Reading teachers are often strong proponents of graphic novels, as Foster discovered: "The reading teachers have been thrilled because the graphic novels are far less intimidating for struggling readers. Yet the graphic novels do not use inferior vocabulary or storytelling. Plus I've noticed some teachers actually recommending them to students when they [the students] say they do not like to read."

While most of your colleagues will accept and acknowledge the success of your graphic novels, not all will realize their application to the curriculum. Most of those we surveyed admitted that teachers generally do not use graphic novels in lessons. A notable exception was pointed out earlier, in the case of Century High School in Maryland, where art teacher Jeff Sharp uses graphic novels from Penny Foster's collection quite extensively. Ms. Foster also has numerous titles in her collection specifically chosen for their curricular connections. This is one way to encourage teachers to use graphic novels: Make sure you have the right books, and then make sure the teachers are aware of them. (Allyson discusses her efforts in this regard in Chapter 1.)

And what about parents? "Parents of the boys who are now embracing chapter books are thrilled," said Resh. Again, success is its own proof and its own defense.

Advice

While this entire book could be considered one big piece of advice to school librarians who wish to incorporate graphic novels into their collections, we thought you would benefit from direct advice from those who have been there. We asked media specialists what advice they would give to their peers:

- "I would advise other media specialists to do the research and get your principal behind you, so that if you encounter resistance, it won't take the principal by surprise. Also, screen the titles carefully. The students are sensitive and parents are sensitive."

- "Graphic novels/comic books are just as valuable in collections as novels. If it gets kids to read and to read for pleasure, which creates life-long readers, I say use the comic books to your advantage."

- "Cover the books with laminate. Not just the spine, the entire book. They last longer and look nicer. Gather all of the books together in one place so they can be easily found, whether they are cataloged 741.5 or fiction. Read as much as you can—reviews *and* the books themselves. Be patient—it may take a while for people to come around and warm up to the idea of graphic novels."

- "Go to your local comic book stores or public library YA section and take a look before you buy."

- "Hook up with someone who is knowledgeable. There are many graphic novels out there that are not appropriate for middle schoolers. I have partnered with a local comic store. He advises me."

- "Do your homework and read the reviews."

- "My advice would be to talk to the kids and see what they are reading. I also did a lot of research on the use of graphic novels in high school. My next move would be to go to a comic store and peruse the books first hand. There is nudity in many that are the level for high school as well as some profanity, which is of course more "graphic" because it is pictured. Seeing the novels before ordering would be helpful. The rep at Diamond [Comic Distributors, Allan Greenberg] was great about cautioning me on some."

- "*Preview!* Find the right material for your audience! It has taken a long time for this medium to gain respect in the library–don't blow it by selecting the fluff and other trash that exists in the comic world *just as in* the traditional collections."

And, last and most enthusiastic:

- "Just do it."
- "Buy them!"

Conclusion

While each experience is obviously unique to the specific situation it embodies, certain issues—content considerations, circulation figures, general acceptance, extraordinary success with boys and reluctant readers—were nigh-universal among those we spoke with.

As you begin to plan your graphic novel collection, bear in mind the experiences of those who have gone before you, always remembering that the standards of your school and community, combined with your expertise and knowledge, come first.

5

Creating Partnerships with Comic Book Stores

As you will see in Chapter 6, there are many, many resources for you to explore and exploit as you begin, maintain, and extend the graphic novel section of your collection. There are distributors, book jobbers, review sources, books, Web sites, listservs, and more. But this chapter is dedicated to a component that merits deeper discussion: The comic book store.

When people who are not familiar with their evolution think about comic books and graphic novels, they tend to rely (understandably) on whatever their personal experience with the medium happens to be. For most Americans, "graphic novel" means "big comic book," and "comic book" equates to the newsstand, drugstore, or convenience store. Most people have memories of ubiquitous wire spinner racks with the bright "HEY, KIDS! COMICS!" sign at the top. Unless you were born after 1980, comic books shared rack space with magazines, candy, and snack chips throughout your formative years.

For the most part, the comic book is no longer available at the local 7-Eleven or newsstand. (For that matter, the local newsstand is almost nonexistent.) The primary outlet for comic books and graphic novels is the comic book specialty store. Graphic novels have made in-roads into bookstores, but comic books themselves are rare in such environs.

What *is* the comic book specialty store? A complete history of its development and evolution is far, *far* beyond the scope of this book. Nor is it necessary for you to have such a complete picture. Suffice it to say that—in general—the comic book specialty store began as a hobby shop devoted to comic books, typically thriving on sales of "back issues" (out-of-print copies of older comic books). In time, as the newsstand market became hostile to comics, the comic book stores became the primary outlet for the comic book industry.

Describing a comic book store is difficult. "A comic book store sells comic books and graphic novels" is an easy way out, but incomplete. Unlike the video, music, or book industries, there are no large national chains in the comic book industry. The thousands of stores in North America that are devoted to selling comic books are independently owned and operated. As a result, each one is unique, reflecting the tastes, opinions, philosophies, and desires of its owner. Comic book store owners, for the most part, are passionate fans of the material they sell. They are a wealth of knowledge, comic book history in human form. Think of it this way: What you are to your students, a comic book store owner can be to you—a wonderful resource.

In case the previous paragraph didn't make it obvious, let us state unequivocally that we think comic book specialty stores are one of the best resources for the media specialist. A well-run, well-loved comic book store is something like an enchanted land, filled with colorful characters and stories, usually stocked with whatever will be the next "big thing" in popular culture. (Comic book stores tend to lead the "big box" stores on things like Pokémon and Yu-Gi-Oh! by six to ten months.)

Comic book stores are such a wonderful resource for you because they are focused almost exclusively on the subject at hand. Yes, you can find graphic novels in many large chain bookstores these days, but the staff there will not, as a rule, have the time or the years of expertise to guide you through the crucial selection process. Just as important: Your average bookstore has to carry hundreds of other kinds of books in addition to graphic novels, whereas a good comic book store will have a truly dizzying selection of graphic novels to choose from (and ready access to any that don't happen to be on the shelves).

Notice that we've said "a good comic book store" several times. Bear in mind what we said above: Comic book stores are independently owned and operated. Most are well-run and professional, usually with a sort of quirky charm that comes from their origins as small businesses. These stores are as good as gold. As with any small or independent business, there are no guarantees, however—you may encounter a store that is not pleasant to deal with or offers little help. This is unfortunate, but there *are* alternatives, which we detail in the next chapter.

But you owe it to yourself to seek out a first-rate comic book store. You can usually find them in your local yellow pages under "Magazines" or "Books." Better yet, you can use the free Comic Shop Locator Service: Just call 1-888-COMIC-BOOK or go to http://csls.diamondcomics.com and enter your zip code. The Service will do the rest.

What follows are two interviews we conducted for the purpose of introducing you to your local comic book store and the best way to interact with its staff. There are thousands of comic book stores in North America alone, and all are different (as we've mentioned), so our intention is to present the alpha and omega of comic book stores. We want to present you with the opinions and ideas of two individuals in the field who are recognized for the general excellence of their businesses and dedication to comics *and* the good that comics can do. Between the two of them, Rory Root (of Comic Relief in Berkeley, California) and Rick Lowell (of Casablanca Comics in the Maine cities of Portland, Windham, and Saco) have close to forty years' experience dealing specifically with schools and libraries with respect to comic books. We chose New England and the Bay Area for the variety that two such distinct regions provide, and spoke to both gentlemen to let them welcome you to your local comic book store.

Interview 1: Rick Lowell

What should a school consider when beginning to use graphic novels in its library?

I guess what needs to be considered is how they intend to use graphic novels. Do they intend to use them as recreational reading? Bringing in reluctant readers who may not be using the library? It might be a case where comics are being used in curriculum. I see them used mostly for recreational reading, though, and I don't think that's a bad thing—it's a great thing. What I'm finding is it's not necessarily your low-end readers who are reading them, but the high-end readers, too.

What are the most popular graphic novels you've seen used in local schools? Why do you think this is the case?

Bone. It's safe for all ages. It has a very strong story and a very clean art style. What I've also found with libraries in general is that they prefer to work with a series rather than a freestanding book. Initially, when I started selling to schools and libraries, my feeling was that I didn't want to get someone committed to a series and potentially overwhelm them. I figured I would deal with freestanding books instead, but the more I talked to them, I realized that series are the way to go. And then, as I began to deal with my own children (who are six and ten at this point and read an unbelievable amount of books!), I saw that they tend to read series: *Magic Treehouse*, *Harry Potter*, *A Series of Unfortunate Events*. Libraries are the same way, so there's no reason not to treat a comic book series the same way. *Bone* is a great example of that. Once you get up into middle and high school, there are more mainstream books that might be more immediately recognizable, such as *Spider-Man* or *Star Wars*, which are also very popular. And maybe some books that aren't quite as recognizable, such as *Akiko* or *Groo*. The thing I love about *Groo* is that it's a series, but at the same time, it's not a series: You can read the books in any order. Plus, it's in color, which makes it more accessible, and it has a lot of humor. But the best thing is that each story has a moral, so if you can show the teacher that last page, where the moral is, the teacher sees that there's substance to it.

What is the best way for a school librarian who is unfamiliar with comics to approach a local store?

There's been a lot of writing in the various trade presses: *School Library Journal*, *VOYA*, and so forth. So if a newcomer can approach a store with at least a list of some of the titles that have been recommended and ask to see those titles, that's a good start. Retailers love to show books off and you're not going in totally blind. Sometimes people come in with very specific lists and that works out well, too, but all you really need is a starting point: the retailer can show them things they might not be aware of. Usually a comic shop isn't going to be as overwhelming as a Borders or a Barnes & Noble in terms of size or atmosphere, but the selection is going to be deeper. And the staff has *read* the books. That's the big difference. When they recommend something, they can give you specific examples of why it may or may not work for you. That's the advantage of the local comic book store. I can tell you why this book or that book may or not be suitable for your audience because I've read them.

For a neophyte in the field, what would you recommend as a core set of books at the elementary, middle, and high school levels?

I'll actually give you the list we show to librarians who come into the store. There's some overlap because some books, for example, are age-appropriate for elementary school but are enjoyed by older kids, too.

Elementary School

Akiko

Archie Americana Series Best of the 80s

Bone

Castle in the Sky

Castle Waiting: Curse of Brambly Hedge

Clan Apis

Groo and Rufferto

Hero Bear and the Kid

Hobbit: An Illustrated Edition

Scary Godmother

Sock Monkey: Glass Doorknob

Spirited Away

Thieves & Kings: Blue Book

Tintin

Usagi Yojimbo

Walt Disney's Comics/Uncle Scrooge

Will Eisner's Last Knight

Will Eisner's Moby Dick

Will Eisner's Princess and the Frog

Will Eisner's Sundiata

Wind in the Willows

Middle School

Akiko

Amazing Spider-Man

Archie Americana Series Best of the 80s

Astro Boy

Batman: No Man's Land

Bone

Books of Magic

Castle in the Sky

Castle Waiting

Daredevil Legends

Dragonball Z

Green Arrow: Quiver

Groo and Rufferto

Hobbit: An Illustrated Edition

Inu Yasha

Joan

Mars

Meridian

Oh My Goddess!

Origin

Ranma ½

Scary Godmother

Simpsons Big Book of Bart Simpson

Spirited Away

Star Wars Dark Empire

Superman & Batman: Generations

Superman for All Seasons

Thieves & Kings

Ultimate Spider-Man

Ultimate X-Men

Usagi Yojimbo

Will Eisner's Last Knight

Will Eisner's Moby Dick

Will Eisner's Princess and the Frog

Will Eisner's Sundiata

Young Justice: A League of Their Own

High School

Amazing Spider-Man

Astro City

Batman: No Man's Land

Batman: The Dark Knight Returns

Batman: The Long Halloween

Blade of the Immortal

Bone

Books of Magic

Castle Waiting

Daredevil Legends

Dragonball Z

Fushigi Yugi

Ghost World

Goodbye Chunky Rice

Green Arrow: Quiver

Groo: All Collections

Hellboy: Chained Coffin & Others

Hobbit: An Illustrated Edition

How to Draw Manga

Inu Yasha

Joan

Kabuki

Mars

Meridian

Oh My Goddess!

Origin

Pedro and Me

Ranma ½

Ruse

Simpsons Big Book of Bart Simpson

Star Wars Dark Empire

Starman

Superman & Batman: Generations   *Ultimate X-Men*
Superman for All Seasons   *Usagi Yojimbo*
The Sandman   *Will Eisner Comics & Sequential Art*
The Tale of One Bad Rat   *Will Eisner Graphic Storytelling*
Ultimate Spider-Man   *Young Justice: A League of Their Own*

In your opinion, what do graphic novels offer a school environment that books do not?

Words and pictures together are a very powerful medium. There are so many kids who love to draw in addition to read. It's an outlet for their imagination. I'll give one example: We did a workshop a couple of months ago where I did a history of comics. Fifty-three kids showed up. The second part of the night was drawing comics. We had 53 kids sitting around drawing comics and *sharing* with each other. There's journal keeping where they have whole notebooks filled with the characters they created and the stories they've developed. It's a tremendous creative outlet for them. They see creating a comic book as something that maybe they can do as well.

Also, graphic novels provide access for reluctant readers, who may not normally use the library. Once they start with graphic novels, they may become more comfortable in the library and start to use other aspects of the library. I was at a school library the other day and the librarian pointed to a particular student and said, "He's read every graphic novel we have, but we never would have seen him in here if we didn't have graphic novels." It was great to stand there talking to her at the checkout counter and while kids came up to return graphic novels because they want to check out the next book in the series. The enthusiasm that I see is very encouraging. They get excited about going to the library. Anything that gets kids excited about going to the library is a good thing.

When did you first start your partnerships with school libraries, and how did you start them?

When I first opened my store in 1987. My aunt is a school librarian and when I first opened my store, she asked me if I could get *Tintin* books for her library. And then I had parents of customers who are librarians and the more we talked, they started to put graphic novels in their libraries and I helped them with that. One year they were talking about the state library conference, and I asked what it was. They explained it to me, so I went and set up a booth, a big booth full of comics and all the librarians walked by me and said, "Why are *you* here?" [*laughs*] I tried to explain that it was because I had something that deserved to be in their library. Honestly, at the time there wasn't nearly as much to show them as there is now, so it was a bit more difficult. But as time has gone on year by year, the librarians who are receptive to implementing graphic novels in their collections have become the best advocates to other librarians. They tell their colleagues, "You have to do this! It works so well!" They're so enthusiastic about. I'm to the point now where I'm dealing with hundreds of libraries on a regular basis.

Why has this happened? A lot of reasons, but I'll mention a buzzword that librarians love to hear: circulation. Buying things for your library that sit there is not the most effective use of your tax dollars or school budget. I went to one of the librarians that I deal with on a regular basis and asked her to give me her circulation figures for the year because she spends a fifth of her YA budget on GN. The director of the library was questioning why such a big chunk on this one category. So I told her to run the figures and show him whether the figures were proportional to what she was spending. Well, she did the figures and for the first nine months of this year [2003], their 471 graphic novels have circulated 3,700 times. Some of these books have been there for a while. Some have plateaued. But still, on average that means that every single graphic novel has gone out eight times this year. That's almost once a month on *everything*. If *every* book was checked out once a month, every month, circulation would be through the roof! Most library books, the popular ones may check out two to three times a year, so there's obviously demand.

What outreach programs have you done for librarians (e.g., presentations)?

Personally, I deal with libraries on an almost daily basis. I'm to the point in my life as a retailer where I have employees who can handle the other aspects of my business and this is the area where I want to focus. So my wife and I do a lot of work with libraries. I do talks on the history of comics. I do a workshop like I described before, where a cartoonist comes in with me and we split the time—I do a history, then he does a cartooning class. I do this in school libraries and classrooms. On Free Comic Book Day, I use the Free Comic Book Day books as donations to libraries. I speak at various conferences, state library conferences, county conferences all over the state—I've been to most of them. I'm on a librarian listserv where I'm sort of an answer man for questions about this. And if I just happen to be passing by a library I've dealt with, I'll stop in to see what's on their shelves and answer any questions.

Don't get me wrong—it's great that I make sales out of this. I make money from it and that's a plus and I won't deny it. But I really just want comics to be as widespread as possible because I've seen how successful they can be and how accepted they've become. And the libraries that have done well with them have done so well that it's astounding.

The biggest outreach is really just keeping the lines of communication open. In March of 2003, in Northampton, Mass., there was the Art of the Book conference. We brought Will Eisner up for that. One of the librarians I deal with on a regular basis is on the board and she wanted to do something special about graphic novels, so she came to me. I told her that she should try to get Will Eisner to speak and she said, "Great! Can you get him?" So I made the call and he accepted, and he was wonderful . Charmed them all and was a wonderful, enthusiastic voice. His *Comics & Sequential Art* and *Graphic Storytelling* should be required in every school library collection, for older kids who are interested in the art form.

What challenges have you faced working with school librarians, and how did you overcome them?

There are several basic arguments I hear all the time, and all of them are easily overcome by simple facts.

First off, some librarians can't even understand why you would want to include graphic novels and you have to explain that it's something that there is an interest in, but also there's storytelling and art aspects.

Second is the argument that no one will check them out. Well, I can disprove that pretty easily! [*laughs*]

Then there's the argument that they're going to be stolen. It's possible, but other things are stolen from libraries, too. I've actually seen very little of it. I've followed up with the librarians who were most concerned about theft, and it turns out that the percentage of loss for graphic novels is no higher than for anything else in the collection.

Finally, there's a concern as to whether or not the books will hold up to repeated checkouts because they're paperbacks, as a rule. Overall, they do hold up. There are a few publishers who need to work on that. But I've seen paperbacks that have circulated twenty, thirty times that are still holding up fine.

Sometimes, just not knowing what to include is a librarian's biggest consideration, and that's where the retailer needs to step up and guide them a little bit.

I've also run into situations, in the past, where I've asked a school librarian, "Do you have graphic novels in your library?" and I'd get the response, "We tried them but they didn't circulate." Well, their idea of "stocking graphic novels" was that they had three of them . . . and they were the wrong three. And they based their entire experience on that. As I say, that was in the past. It really isn't an issue now.

As with any collection, you have to have a critical mass before it becomes accepted and successful. Three books is not a graphic novel collection. Ten books is maybe the beginning of a graphic novel collection. You don't have to do it all at once. You can do it bit by bit. But you wouldn't go into a library that has a video collection and see *Forrest Gump* and *Casablanca* as the only two videos and think that they have a video collection! Same thing with graphic novels.

I think librarians need to realize what the costs are and what needs to be done to get started. I think they can get at least a good beginning collection for under $200.00. But they need to realize that it's not a one-time purpose. If you're going to make a commitment to it, plan on replenishing your collection whenever it is you replenish books. Because you'll get your graphic novels and eventually you'll reach a plateau where the kids who are going to read those books have read them all and they're going to want something else, and if you don't have something else, you're not going to get new readers and the ones who were using your library are going to go away, too. It's an ongoing process.

What has been the most requested title from schools?

Well, *Bone* because I've preached it so heavily. But also *Maus* at the high school level. Sometimes things that they'll see in *School Library Journal* become extremely popular. Here's the best example: Last year, *SLJ* did an article on the thirty graphic novels every school library should have. I got a call from a new school library customer and she gave me that list. I didn't know about the article at the time, so I just took it as a list. It was a very specific list and I was a little surprised to see it from someone new to graphic novels, but it was a good list, so I figured she had asked around and done her research. I put the order together. The next day, I had another librarian with the exact same list! I thought, "Well, OK, they must have talked to the same people." Within a week, I had twenty librarians using the same list! I finally asked where the list had come from and they told me. They were all using the same list, which is fine up to a point.

I say up to a point because I have three issues with published lists: 1) What may be appropriate for an elementary school in Maine may not be appropriate for an elementary school in, say, Kansas. Community standards have to come into account. 2) The recommendation of material that is no longer in print, which is maddening. 3) Sometimes there will be heavy slants toward particular publishers. There are books that I like that I think are important, worthy books, but they won't circulate. It can make a list, but not necessarily ever check out. I hate to single out any particular example, but there have been a couple of books—*great* books—that have made it onto a number of lists, and a lot of librarians put them on the shelves and then come to me and say, "This book hasn't gone out once." And I could have told them, if they'd asked, that that book would never circulate. If you can afford to put a great book in your library just because it's a great book, fine, but most libraries can't do that. That's the danger of just taking someone else's list and placing an order. You should really walk into the store, talk to the people there, look at the book yourself. To blindly follow a list is dangerous.

What has been the most often cited reason for using graphic novels that librarians have given you?

In my situation, it's because they've talked to the other librarians who've already done it and they're saying, "You have *got* to do this." For example, I have a librarian in my local school district who's such a strong advocate of using graphic novels that she's basically talked to every other librarian in the district. She's had comic book days, she's had parties where the kids all come in and read after school. Took a class trip to see *Spider-Man*. But it's one librarian telling another "I've had success with this. It's something you should look at." That along with the amount of press it's been getting lately. I think some people have been worn down by the amount of press. If you read about graphic novels once, you think, "Well, OK, maybe," but when you read every single month that this is something libraries are using and having success with, you start to realize you need to look into this! Plus the kids are all asking for it, because they've discovered the Japanese comics on the Internet and they've become interested in the art form.

Are you willing to work with school libraries regarding payment and shipping?

      Absolutely. We do a 20% discount with free shipping and unlimited consultation. Whatever they need. Most of them work with purchase orders and that's not a problem. Purchase orders are fine. Sometimes Net 30 days becomes Net 60, then Net 90, but we work with them.

What should the school librarian know before she ventures forth into the comic book industry?

      I hate to speak for other shops, but I guess I would say be aware that despite the perception that it's a predominantly male-oriented industry, there's great deal of material available for women. Most people of think of comics and they think of Archie, or superheroes. There's more than that. There are so many thousands of graphic novels that a librarian should be able to find something that works for her.

Interview 2: Rory Root

What should a school consider when beginning to use graphic novels in its library?

Well, number one is understanding how graphic novels support their mission. Is the goal to support sustained silent reading? Is it to support curriculum? Is it to provide fun entertaining reading? Is it to provide another avenue to reach reluctant readers, as a way to get them to discover the joy of reading? There are a number of things graphic novels can do to help in each of these causes and a library's collection would be built differently to support each, or all, of these different missions. So, know from the beginning what you're trying to accomplish—it helps when you try to figure out if you've actually gotten there!

What are the most popular graphic novels you've seen used in local schools? Why do you think this is the case?

It depends on what level of school you're talking about. Obviously the books one would select for K–6 would be different than junior high school or middle school, which would be different from high schools. High schools in particular can vary wildly because of the diversity between grades 9–12, both in the audience that the libraries are serving *and* in the various reading levels and skills that the students bring to the table. It really does vary on a school and age setting, and very much by community. Probably the single most installed graphic novel is *Maus* by Art Spiegelman, Pulitzer Prize winner from 1992. It's required reading in a number of ninth and tenth grade levels, and even in some junior high schools in California. It's probably one of the most collected graphic novels in school library systems. Others tend to be books such as *Bone*, which is a great light-hearted high fantasy romp by Jeff Smith. Another is a book called *The Tale of One Bad Rat* [a frank depiction of the effects and damage of child abuse], which tends to be more in private school libraries, or high school libraries where they understand that visceral subjects often do belong in the library system. Some communities don't support a librarian or teacher looking to bring material for at-risk youth into the school system. They tend to think it might glorify or just bring the subject up. *Tale of One Bad Rat* is probably one of the most collected books in the public library system. We've had very erratic results here with school systems, some wanting it and loving it. It's a fantastic story and unfortunately because of communities or school administrators or parents, some schools have difficulty with that being in their collections. Others find it especially useful and appropriate.

What is the best way for a school librarian who is unfamiliar with comics to approach a local store?

One: please call ahead for an appointment. Talk to the owner or manager. There are a couple of days in the week that are generally bad for a comic book store to serve its library clientele, with Wednesdays in particular being new comic book day (sometimes Thursday when Monday is a holiday), Saturdays are also problematic. You don't want to come in on a Wednesday during lunch rush and expect to receive their best and most attentive service. You'll get as much help as we can give you, but we actually prefer to have librarians come in on a Monday or Tuesday, before or after normal shop hours. My staff and I have worked with librarians for sixteen years now. We speak librarian to some degree; we know what some of their concerns and needs are. Librarians and comic store staffs each have their own jargon, and sometimes the two don't easily mesh. I've been doing this a long time and I'm a lifetime reader in the Berkeley library system, a library tech in high school. I know my way around the Dewey Decimal system. I know my way around a lot of library issues, but I'm still learning. I'm a member of BAYA (a Bay Area young adult group). I've spoken at CCI (California Children's Institute) and CLA (California Library Association) as well as the ALA and ABA/BEA. I think I know how to introduce librarians to graphic novels, but my favorite way is *in situ.* We can bring them into the store; show them the 9,000 volumes we have here (that's by title, not by quantity). This gives the librarian some idea of the diversity that comics have to offer. Also, the trades—*School Library Journal, Library Journal, VOYA,* and *Today's Librarian*—all have had articles on graphic novels and collection building. There's a phenomenal resource called GN-LIB Topica, which is one of the listservs for librarians with over 500 librarians on that listserv, and in the archives there's a remarkable wealth of recommended titles, of issues to be aware of. It's a great peer resource. Also, Comic Relief offers two catalogs. One is a general audience catalog for mostly public libraries and the other is more targeted toward middle schools. Both are age-coded and genre-coded, and both only collect titles that have actually sold into multiple library systems. So there's a sense of peer review in the catalog. But no catalog can substitute for putting a book in your hands, looking through it and judging for yourself whether it belongs in your collection.

For a neophyte in the field, what would you recommend as a core set of books at the elementary, middle, and high school levels?

Primary School

Bone

The Essentials Series (from Marvel Comics)

Akiko

Bart Simpson Collections

Archie

Disney Comics (*Uncle Scrooge*, etc.)

Marvels

Asterix

Hero Bear and the Kid

Leave It to Chance

Batman Adventures

The Power Puff Girls

Yu Gi Oh

Middle School

Bone

Persepollis

Tintin

The Simpsons collections

Elfquest

The Tale of One Bad Rat

Dragonball

Love Hina

Star Wars

Kare Kano

Clan Apis

Sandwalk Adventure

High School

Ranma ½

Maus

Watchmen

Ghost World

Sandman

Nausicaa

Contract with God

Batman: The Dark Knight Returns

Chobits

Gonick's Cartoon History of the Universe

Safe Area Gorazde

A few recommended Reference Books: *The Slings & Arrows Comics Guide* (a review/reference work for over 5,000 titles), *Understanding Comics* by Scott McCloud, Will Eisner's *Comics & Sequential Art, The Overstreet Comic Price Guide* (very useful for dates and creator notes), *Bridgman's Anatomy,* the *Hogarth Anatomy* series, *How to Draw Manga, Panel One* (script samples for comics), *How to Draw Comics the Marvel Way* (excellent lessons on perspective), *DC's Guides to Writing and Drawing,* and *Dark Horse's Guide to Inking.*

In your opinion, what do graphic novels offer a school environment that other books do not?

Foremost, they offer a pathway to find the joy of reading. I myself have been a lifelong reader and I wouldn't attribute this to comics by any means, but they certainly helped. If somebody finds what it is that they want to read, whether it's Romance novels, Mysteries, Science Fiction, Westerns, Histories, or Comics, you can't stop them. And the pathway to reading for a number of people who had previously missed the joy of reading has been comic books. Another thing they offer is curriculum enhancement. At the California Children's Institute, I once heard a doctor from St. Louis talk about the growth of synapses in the brain and how at the junior high school level, it's often a use-it-or-lose it scenario, where synaptic patterns that were established as a child start to atrophy if they're not reinforced. Now, I believe that all right-brain/left-brain analogies are somewhat suspect physiologically, but perhaps this analogy will stand: visual storytelling is often referred to as right-brain material, while textual storytelling is often left-brain material. Combine the two (as comics do) and this causes the two hemispheres to synthesize one meaning out of a combined picture; which 1) is challenging if it's not already learned behavior, and 2) provides a different method for some curricular material to enter students' thoughts. You're teaching kids new ways to think. A number of graphic novels can give kids a new perspective on history, like *Age of Bronze* by Eric Shanower, a wonderfully researched story of *The Iliad*. It has an incredible bibliography, directing you to other books detailing the legends of this great history and mythology and I think it's a great read too. I would recommend it for a high school level because I don't think many junior high school kids or elementary kids would appreciate the depth of storytelling going on there, and I'm not sure their parents would appreciate some of the historically accurate portrayal of Greek life in those days!

When did you first start your partnerships with school libraries, and how did you start those partnerships?

It was 16 years ago that the Berkeley Public Library started to use us extensively for collection building and to start a graphic novel-specific collection. About a year after that—through word-of-mouth—some of the school librarians started coming in and picking up particular books, sometimes on a student request, sometimes on their own initiative. And it snowballed from there.

What outreach programs have you done for librarians (e.g., presentations)?

We do booktalks. We've done workshops with BAYA, CCI. I just did a presentation of manga and anime for Bay Net for an audience comprised mostly of school librarians, many of whom came right over to Comic Relief all fired up to see more, some with their credit cards at the ready! Always a heartwarming experience for a bookseller.

Some school systems are locked into buying from certain institutional vendors, such as B&T or BWI. I understand that we're not going to have every comic book dollar come our way, nor should we. But you should use your local resources, whether it be Comic Relief in Berkeley, California, Casablanca Comics in Maine, Jim Hanley's Universe in New York, Bedrock City in Houston, or Golden Apple in Los Angeles (these are some of the stores that I know work well with libraries), or the store around the corner from your school. Also by building up local resources, librarians have access to the community of comics as a whole. It's useful if you're looking for artists to do a chalk talk, or to come in and diagram how a comic book is made for a fifth grade class and then teach that class how to make their own comic books. The local comic book store can be a great resource. Plus, they know your community standards. They know what's popular in the area. They also know what may be problematical in the area. They may have worked with the library down the street, whether it's public, private, or school.

So would you say that even if you have to buy somewhere else, the local comic book store is still the place to go to put your hands on the books and to learn?

With one caveat: if that's what you're going to do, let the store know up-front. Nothing's more frustrating than to walk someone through a $25,000.00 order and have administration move it to BWI instead of your bookstore.

There are good comic stores and there are comic stores that could, shall we say, be better. Finding the appropriate comic store is really important. There are several hundred stores in the Bay Area, many of which are national award winners, but I believe we handle a large proportion of the library business locally because, as I say, we speak librarian, and we speak comic book. It's just a question of finding the store that works for your particular situation. If the first comic book store that a librarian walks into says, "Hey, this ain't a library, kid!" when she picks a book up off the shelf, she's found the wrong store! And she needs to go find the right one. Call first; make an appointment to explain what you're doing. If you want to use the store as a resource and not as a buying source, let them know up-front. Most of the time, a shop won't mind donating its time as long as it knows up-front that it's donating the time!

Sometimes, school librarians don't have the choice: administration or contracts dictate that they buy elsewhere. Now, one time I had a school system place an order with another outfit and request that it be sourced through us since we had helped them. This was a case where they had to buy from Source X, but they wanted to help us. I figured it would never happen, but it actually worked out—Source X bought the product from us, to my surprise and delight.

What challenges have you faced working with school librarians, and how did you overcome them?

There are a number of issues. You find that some administrations, some teachers, some parents, some fellow librarians, even, look at comics as a lesser literature. Overcoming their preconceptions about what graphic novels have to offer to the system can be a challenge. Frankly, to paraphrase Harvey Pekar: "We revere words; we devote libraries to house them. We adore pictures; we build museums to house them. Somehow when you combine the two, we're talking something for dunces and dunderheads." There is a preconception that comics are a lesser literature, a bowdlerized literature, that they're not for the best and brightest, yet surveys of comic book readers show that they have incredibly enhanced vocabularies thanks to the comics, that they found a love of reading, that they read beyond comics, that they read for pleasure, for entertainment, and for information. The statistics for comic readership are great.

Some librarians are concerned about "one-circ" issues: the book is checked out once and never comes back. That was a problem early on with some collections that had single issues of comic books, but it's not been a real problem with graphic novels. It happens, but then again, it happens with other library materials, too, whether it's DVDs, CDs, or general fiction. It's not the problem some people seem to think it will be.

For circulation issues in general: Most of the statistics I have come from public libraries, but these are books that circulate thirty, forty, fifty times a year, when (by comparison) a national fiction best seller might circulate five times a year. (*Harry Potter* aside, of course!) It's just phenomenal circulation figures. At the Asian branch of the Oakland Public Library, circulation jumped 1,400% two years ago and they attribute half of that increase to having graphic novels in their branch.

In terms of other problems school libraries have: Sometimes it's finding age-appropriate material. A lot of comics that the staff of a comic book store might find personally thrilling or entertaining are written beyond what would be comfortable in some school library collections. So one needs to be careful to winnow for appropriate content.

The only long-term problem we've really had is in libraries being properly funded. Some have had remarkably effective parent groups that have come in with donations of a couple hundred or even a few thousand dollars here and there. One of the local private schools comes in about every three to four months, spending one to two thousand dollars, all money raised by parents. That's useful, and the parents are seeing real value to their students.

One more thing that should be brought up: Bindery issues. Graphic novels are often bound with small gutters, so if you have them rebound (as schools often do), you can lose or pinch some of the art. Early on, some graphic novels from some publishers used weaker glue and had a tendency to get damaged if they weren't treated properly (and as we know, not everyone treats books properly!). But for the most part, the newer formats use better glues and suffer less from bindery issues. If a school has a problem with it, they should talk to the vendor and also go past the vendor and speak directly to the publisher as well.

What has been the most requested title from schools?

In the older days, absolutely *Maus*, but at this point, I think *Maus* is in just about every school library! [*laughs*] Right now, probably *Bone*. After *Bone*, it really starts to vary based on school system.

One of the things that the recent boom in manga and anime has caused is a relationship between animation and circulation building. If an animated series is running on Cartoon Network, for example, and there's a related manga, the kids want it.

What has been the most often cited reason for using graphic novels that school librarians have given you?

Peer recommendations. We had a number of early pioneers fifteen–twenty years ago, but right now, they've been reading for the last few years in sources like *School Library Journal* that they should be doing this, and either the administration finally caved [*laughs*] or they finally got around to it. Oftentimes, we'll find that the librarian him or herself is a bit reticent, but since they've heard so much about it, they figure "Let's take a look." More often than not, they have a conception of what comics are, and we get them in the store and start walking them around, showing them the various titles, and it's a lot of fun to watch their eyes open up as they say, "I had no idea this kind of graphic novel was available." A great example: *Goodbye, Chunky Rice*. What a wonderful book. A librarian came in; she had never bought comics before. She had $300 to spend out of a $1200 allocation and darned if she didn't end up spending all $1200 here! She later came back and bought five copies of *Goodbye, Chunky Rice* to give to her friends. It's perfect for high school.

Also, the explosion in manga, its enormous popularity, is one of the things that have probably brought in a lot of librarians who until now have resisted the siren call of comics.

Are you willing to work with school libraries regarding payment and shipping?

We work the way they like us to work! We'll take a purchase order. Now, some librarians like to show up unannounced on a Friday evening and wipe out our shelves. No! Bad librarian, no biscuit! [*laughs*] Please give us a call and make an appointment so we can serve you properly. We'll show you the books in person, or we'll work through catalogs and e-mail lists. You place the order with us; we'll place it with our vendors.

Librarians should also be aware of their own payment systems. If your school is paying Net 90 Days, as much as you might want to patronize that comic book store down the street, realize that that store might not be able to afford to tie up that much inventory without payment for 90 days. Talk to them. Explain what the system is. Talk to the administration to get details. We've had some librarians who've wanted the books so badly that they come in and put it on a credit card, trusting that the school system will pay them back relatively soon. That said, we prefer to work with P.O.s. You come in, pick out the books you want, we write them up and give you a total and a pro forma invoice. Then we can reshelve them, you give us your P.O. and we place the order with our vendors. When the books come in, we get them to you and you pay us in 30–45 days. Reality is often 45–90 days. One system took six months to pay for a large order. That hurt! Some systems are slow to pay, some are quick; know which you are and inform your source for books. The local comic shop may not be conversant with working with purchase orders, so talk to them. At Comic Relief, we know that P.O.s from the local school are as good as gold, but some stores will need to be reassured. It's important that the store realizes that they *will* get paid so that they don't think something's gone wrong. Sometimes the comic book store won't know to ask about this sort of thing, and it would be bad to sour what should be a great relationship over this sort of misunderstanding.

Summary

The local comic book store can serve multiple purposes for the school librarian. A local store is a wealth of information on the topic at hand. The staff of such a store can make recommendations, point out new titles of interest, and, in short, act as a guide for even an experienced educator through the sometimes bewildering maze of available graphic novels. Better yet, since comic book stores are independently owned and operated by members of the community, the staff knows and understands the community standards, a great help to the school librarian who must keep such things in mind. A comic book store, therefore, is not only a source of the product itself, but also a source of information *about* the product.

Resources and Support

This book exists to help you institute a policy of using graphic novels in your collection. It provides you with the resources and rationale to locate graphic novels, evaluate them, purchase them, and—when necessary—justify them to parents, colleagues, and supervisors.

But there is a vast wealth of information about comic books and graphic novels available. If, like most newcomers to graphic novels, you find yourself becoming a fan of them, you'll want to learn more. Just as likely is that your students will clamor for more information, more graphic novels, more news about them, more everything!

As we've mentioned before, there are literally *thousands* of graphic novels in print, with more published every month. There are volumes written on the history of comic books, the development of the art form, the theories that underlie it, and the ways to manipulate it. There are review sources and biographies and indexes and more—in short, everything you'd expect in any thriving field of artistic endeavor.

This chapter points you toward these resources and other forms of support. Some are specific to schools and libraries, while others are nonspecific. All are focused on comic books and graphic novels, and have something to offer to students . . . and those who teach them.

Authors' note: In the interest of full disclosure, we note here that Barry is employed by Diamond Comic Distributors, mentioned below, and is involved in the administration of Free Comic Book Day, also mentioned below.

Section 1: How to Buy Graphic Novels

Comic Book Specialty Stores

In Chapter 5 you met two comic book retailers and learned a bit about the comic book specialty store. There are a couple of ways to find a comic book store in your area:

1. **Use your local yellow pages.** Usually, comic book stores are listed under "Booksellers" and/or "Magazine stores."

2. **Go to The Master List (www.the-master-list.com)**, a free listing of comic book stores in the United States, Canada, and around the world. The Master List's strength goes beyond its listings of stores: There are also consumer reviews of each shop, basic information on ordering comics, and a helpful FAQ.

3. **Use the Comic Shop Locator Service (CSLS)**, a free service of Diamond Comic Distributors (see below for more information on Diamond). The CSLS can be accessed by phone (888-COMIC-BOOK) or online (csls.diamondcomics.com). Punch in your zip code and you will get a list of stores in the area. Each store has the option of producing a store profile, which can tell you more about the store and also includes a map to its location. The CSLS lists stores in the United States, Canada, and around the world. Participation is voluntary and is limited to stores that do business with Diamond (which is most of them).

While we recommend using a local comic book store for your purchases, we understand that this is not always possible or practical. Listed in the following section are other sources for graphic novels.

Book Jobbers That Carry Graphic Novels

You will most likely be familiar with most of the names listed below, as they are standard book jobbers used by school librarians for years.

The benefits of a book jobber can be many: By adding your graphic novel purchases to your regular order, you may receive a higher discount. The book jobber knows and understands your needs already. Also, several book jobbers will provide MARC records and process the graphic novels according to your specifications, which comic book stores and distributors are not equipped to do.

Baker & Taylor
http://www.btol.com/index.cfm
btinfo@btol.com
800-775-1800

Book House, Inc.
http://www.thebookhouse.com/
800-248-1146

Book Wholesalers, Inc.
http://www.bwibooks.com/index.php
800-888-4478

Brodart
http://www.brodart.com
bookinfo@brodart.com
800-233-8467

Demco Media
http://www.demcomedia.com
turtleback@demcomedia.com
800-448-8939

Follett Library Resources
http://www.follett.com/
customerservice@flr.follett.com
888-511-5114

Ingram Book
http://www.ingrambook.com/home.htm
info@ingrambook.com
800-937-8000

Koen Book Distributors
http://www.koen.com/
info@koen.com
800-257-8481

Perma-Bound Books
http://www.perma-bound.com
books@perma-bound.com
800-637-6581

Regent Book Company
http://regentbook.com/
info@regentbook.com
800-999-9554

Diamond Comic Distributors

Diamond Comic Distributors
http://www.diamondcomics.com
library@diamondcomics.com
800-45-COMIC

Diamond is "the world's largest distributor of English-language comic books, graphic novels, and related pop culture merchandise." The company sells graphic novels to thousands of comic book specialty stores worldwide and maintains exclusive relationships with a number of publishers. Diamond also sells graphic novels to bookstores and book jobbers (such as those listed above). The company also sells direct to school libraries.

Diamond maintains a Web site dedicated to schools and libraries called The Diamond Bookshelf, located online at http://bookshelf.diamondcomics.com. The site lists thousands of graphic novels, categorized by age level and genre, with Dewey classifications and subjects. (Diamond also publishes a print catalog with several dozen high-profile titles. The catalog is available for free by contacting the company.)

The Bookshelf also includes monthly graphic novel reviews by professional reviewer and librarian Kat Kan.

Section 2: Book Binderies for Softcover Graphic Novels

In our experience, graphic novels (whether hardcover or softcover) hold up under continued usage just as well as any other bound printed matter. It is true that, in the past, there were some issues regarding binding that caused graphic novels to deteriorate more quickly than other books. In recent years, though, publishers have heard the pleas of librarians and have improved their glues and binding processes.

Barry was surprised, then, when a media specialist approached him at a recent convention for school librarians and told him that her graphic novels were falling apart.

After some discussion, the culprit became apparent: The graphic novels were circulating so much that they were getting the equivalent of a year's worth of wear in a month or so! No wonder their wear and tear had accelerated.

In general, then, graphic novels are as hardy as your other books but, like *any* product, repeated use beyond the norm will begin to take its toll. If this ends up being the case, then you may want to investigate book binding to stretch your purchasing dollars.

Of course, you may want to investigate book binding in any event, as publishers do not offer library binding at this time. There are many companies that will bind your books for added durability or to keep your graphic novels consistent with other books in your collection.

Authors' note: We do recommend that you examine each book carefully before having it bound and be certain that you speak to the binding folks about the process: As Rory Root mentions in Chapter 5, graphic novels tend to have a shallower printing gutter than most books (to maximize the artwork), and a bad binding job can cut off some of the images . . . and the story!

Following are companies that bind graphic novels:

Acme Bookbinding
http://www.acmebook.com/
100 Cambridge St.
Charlestown, MA 02129-0004
Phone: 800-242-1821
Fax: 617-242-3764
Contact Phone: 617-242-1100

Arizona Library Binding Company
1337 W. McKinley
Phoenix, AZ 85007
Phone: 602-253-1861
Fax: 602-253-1863

Bridgeport National Bindery Inc.
http://www.bnbindery.com/
104 Ramah Circle S. / PO Box 289
Agawam, MA 01001-0289
Phone: 800-223-5083
Fax: 413-789-4007

The Heckman Bindery, Inc.
http://www.boundtoplease.com/
1010 N. Sycamore St.
North Manchester, IN 46962
Phone: 800-334-3628
Fax: 219-982-1104

Lehmann Bookbinding, Ltd.
http://www.lehmannbookbinding.com/
97 Ardelt Ave.
Kitchener, ONT N2C 2E1
CANADA
Phone: 800-4633573
Fax: 519-570-4452
Contact Phone: 519-570-4444

Milford Bookbinding, Inc.
3723 S. Highway 99
Stockton, CA 95215
Phone: 209-941-2085
Fax: 209-941-0401

Ocker & Trapp/Library Bindery, Inc.
http://www.ockerandtrapp.com/
17C Palisada Ave.
Emerson, NJ 07630-0229
Phone: 800-253-0262
Fax: 201-265-0588
Contact Phone: 201-265-0262

Wert Bookbinding, Inc.
http://www.wertbookbinding.com
9975 Allentown Blvd.
Grantville, PA 17028
Phone: 800-344-9378
Fax: 717-469-0629

Section 3: Information Specific to Schools/School Libraries

There are many resources available regarding graphic novels, but those in this section are particularly suited to school librarians looking for help, information, and guidance on graphic novels.

Comics in Education

http://home.earthlink.net/%7Egeneyang/comicsedu/index.html

A great site that makes connections between education and the world of comic books and graphic novels. Of particular note are its section recounting the history of comics in education and its excellent bibliography. Use this site as a reference tool to defend your inclusion of graphic novels in your collection, should you need to.

GN-Lib

GN-Lib is the "Graphic Novels for Librarians" listserv, maintained on the Topica Web site (www.topica.com/lists). A heavily trafficked listserv, it boasts a membership in the hundreds, composed of comic book retailers, public librarians, and school librarians. Its purpose is to trade information and advice on using graphic novels in any library setting, and it's a terrific resource for the newbie who has questions about doing so. To subscribe to the list, send an e-mail to gnlib-l-subscribe@topica.com.

Graphic Novels: A Bibliographic Guide to Book-Length Comics

A publication of Libraries Unlimited, D. Aviva Rothschild's book (published in 1995) was the first annotated guide of its type, listing more than 400 graphic novels and commenting on style, quality, stories, and more. The guide is slanted toward the book and library markets, as opposed to the comic book market, making it a valuable resource for school librarians.

Powell's Books

http://www.powells.com/psection/GraphicNovels.html

Powell's Books is an e-tailer of books with a wonderful collection of graphic novels, including cover images, story synopses, publishers' comments, and reviews. Better yet, the site offers Sears subjects and lists other graphic novels for further reading. Of particular interest is the weekly Top Ten list, spelling out the top-selling titles of the week at Powell's—a great way to gauge potential interest. A great resource for research on the newest titles or for purchasing purposes.

Recommended Graphic Novels for Public Libraries (selected and annotated by Steve Raiteri)

http://my.voyager.net/~sraiteri/graphicnovels.htm

Steve Raiteri, a public librarian from Ohio, has been reading comic books and graphic novels for the past twenty-five years and has incorporated them into his public library collection. The site lists titles that are appropriate for a young adult collection as well as information about starter collections, Web sites of publishers, and links pertaining to the graphic novel industry. Latest editions appear in red for quick reference. Currently, Raiteri writes graphic novel reviews for *Library Journal.*

Section 4: General Information about Graphic Novels—Online/Electronic

Once you've exhausted the sources of information devoted specifically to school and school libraries, you'll probably want to branch out into the wider world of comic books and graphic novels. The following online resources are excellent repositories of information about comics, whether they discuss the history of the medium, its status as art, the latest and greatest (or upcoming) titles, or any combination of the above.

Comic Book Resources: http://www.comicbookresources.com

Newsarama: http://www.newsarama.com

The Pulse: http://www.comicon.com/pulse

Silver Bullet Comic Books: http://www.silverbulletcomicbooks.com

The number of Web sites devoted to the comic book industry from the perspective of industry insiders and long-time fans is enormous, but these four are among the most-traveled and, taken in concert, most comprehensive informational resources on modern comics in general. Each has regular news updates, interviews with comic book creators, reviews of new titles, previews of upcoming books, and more. Each also has its own character and, of course, its own strengths and weaknesses.

Be aware that these sites are designed and developed *by* comic book fans *for* comic book fans. While all are good sources of information, some content presupposes a certain level of knowledge. Realize that reviews on these sites are typically designed to let fans know if the latest title is "cool" or not, not written as a tool for you to use to determine worthiness for inclusion in your collection. (See Section 7 below for review sources.)

Due to the nature of the Internet, message board chat on these sites can be rowdy and impassioned. It can also be informative. These sites and others like them can be an educational experience for the school librarian interested in graphic novels, but bear in mind that, unless you are a regular reader of comics already, they are not designed with you in mind.

Amazon.com

http://www.amazon.com/graphicnovels

Amazon.com has a section devoted to graphic novels at this URL. In addition to listing top-selling, popular titles (broken down into genre categories), Amazon also lists its recent best sellers, a great way to gauge potential interest.

Comic Book Legal Defense Fund

http://www.cbldf.org

Due to their images and their history as a "children's" medium, comic books are particularly vulnerable to censorship. A typical layperson's attitude is that the medium is designed, dedicated, and intended for children and children alone. Consequently, the slightest whiff of mature content can be enough to set off censors' alarms.

Comics have a nasty past when it comes to censorship. While a complete recounting of events is beyond the purview of this book, suffice it to say that the comics industry is extremely sensitive to censorship, both real and perceived. In the 1950s, an overreaction by the U.S. Congress resulted in comics censoring themselves rather than submitting to government scrutiny and censorship. The results of this decision still echo today, as the perception that "comics are for kids" comes largely from this period of creating comics that were as innocuous as possible.

To protect itself from future censorship, the industry supports the Comic Book Legal Defense Fund (CBLDF), an organization dedicated to protecting the First Amendment rights of comic book creators and those who sell comics.

As librarians, media specialists, and teacher librarians, we are used to defending our choices, books being challenged, and falling prey to censors. If you use graphic novels in your collection, consider supporting the CBLDF. It is as vital as defending any other book on your shelves.

The Comics Journal

http://www.tcj.com

The online presence for *The Comics Journal*, the comic book world's premier arts magazine. Selected content from the print magazine is reproduced on the Web site, along with a daily Web log and monthly audio archives of the *Journal*'s legendary, exhaustive interviews with top creators from every era of comics history.

Free Comic Book Day

http://www.freecomicbookday.com

More than a Web site, Free Comic Book Day is an event in and of itself. Once a year, the comic book industry comes together and gives away millions of free comic books in thousands of comic book specialty shops around the country. This site is dedicated to the event, which aims to remind people of the power and promise of the comic book art form. As a result, it contains pages and pages of information on the history of comics, including lists of important dates in comics history, the first appearances of certain characters, and generally all the information a newcomer to comics might need to begin to understand them.

In addition, Free Comic Book Day offers school librarians an opportunity to plug into the larger comic book community. The event's organizers typically involve public and school libraries in the event, usually by matching them up with local stores, which sponsor the libraries for the event. A school library can participate in Free Comic Book Day, get free comics, and help promote comics in the school (and literacy) all in one fell swoop. Free Comic Book Day is endorsed by literacy organization Get Caught Reading.

The History Channel's *Comic Book Superheroes Unmasked*

By far the best tool for newcomers to the world of comic books we've seen in recent years is *Comic Book Superheroes Unmasked*, a two-hour documentary that The History Channel aired in the summer of 2003. Meticulously researched, compellingly presented, and rife with interesting details and tidbits, the special examines the history of comic books from the debut of Superman in 1938 to the present, and includes on-air interviews with legends from just about every era of comics. As the show's title indicates, it focuses on superheroes and therefore pays less attention to other genres, but since superheroes have been a part of comics almost since the beginning, telling their history also tells the history of the medium itself. Even stalwart comic book readers were impressed by the detail and scholarship in the special; for newcomers it's a fast, phenomenal introduction to the world of comics.

The special is available on VHS tape and DVD from the A&E Store, online at http://store.aetv.com. Best of all, once you purchase the program, The History Channel permits you to use it for nonprofit educational purposes, meaning that it can also be aired as part of a lesson or for research purposes in your media center.

Wikipedia: The Free Encyclopedia

http://en2.wikipedia.org/wiki/Graphic_novel

This electronic encyclopedia offers a fine definition of a graphic novel and discusses the components, style, and writing of the same, along with examples and links to online resources. This Web site is a quick, perfect way to introduce graphic novels to faculty, students, or the community.

Section 5: General Information about Graphic Novels—In Print

The Comics Journal. **Seattle, WA: Fantagraphics Books, 1976.**

The Comics Journal approaches comics from an art-criticism perspective, offering retrospectives and critiques of the very best in the medium. Over the years the magazine's stance has made it many foes in the industry. The magazine's Web site says it best: "Despite a contentious relationship with the rest of the North American comics industry, due in no small part to its investigative news stories and uncompromising review section, the *Journal* has won several industry awards, most notably multiple recent wins in the Eisner and Harvey ceremonies" (www.tcj.com).

Comics and Sequential Art. **Will Eisner.** Tamarac, FL: Poorhouse Press, 1994.
Graphic Storytelling & Visual Narrative. **Will Eisner.** Tamarac, FL: Poorhouse Press, 1996.

Eisner began his career as a comic book creator during the Golden Age of comics and continues to produce powerful, viable work to this day. In these two books, he puts a lifetime's experience in comics on paper, discussing and developing the theories that underlie the creation of graphic novels. A true pioneer, Eisner was one of the first to take this particular approach to graphic novels, setting forth a theoretical framework for other generations to follow. These books are recommended for advanced students or those with an interest in art theory.

101 Best Graphic Novels. **Stephen Weiner.** New York: NBM Publishing, Inc., 2003.

Originally developed as a guide for public libraries (the author is a librarian), this book has evolved into an excellent resource for anyone who is looking for top-notch selections for a new graphic novel collection.

The Overstreet Comic Book Price Guide. **Robert M. Overstreet, et al.** Timonium, MD: Gemstone Publishing, 1970– . Annual.

Each year for more than three decades, Robert Overstreet has compiled his *Price Guide*, considered by many to be the bible of comic book values, with prices listed for thousands of titles in a variety of conditions. While the pricing information is suited for avid collectors (who buy and sell their comics and care deeply about each title's condition), its main value to the school librarian rests in its informative articles on the history of comics, profiles of certain creators and titles, and more. The prices themselves can even be used to teach lessons in supply and demand, inflation, and general collecting concepts.

Reinventing Comics: How Imagination and Technology Are Revolutionizing an Art Form. **Scott McCloud.** New York: DC Comics/Paradox Press, 2000.
Understanding Comics. **Scott McCloud.** New York: DC Comics/Paradox Press, 1994.

Comic book creator Scott McCloud's *Understanding Comics* was a watershed publication in the history of comics, using Eisner's theories and applying them to art throughout history in an attempt to do more than simply explain how and why comics work. McCloud sought to explain what comics *were* at their most basic level, and what made them so distinct from other media. His follow-up work, *Reinventing Comics*, examines the technological revolution and business aspects of modern comics, laying the groundwork for educated discussion on what forms graphic novels may take in the future.

Understanding Comics is highly theoretical, but its very nature (the whole book is written as a graphic novel) makes it accessible to any reader. It is deep and theoretical, but an excellent way for the curious student (or teacher!) to learn more about graphic novels. *Reinventing Comics*, with its focus on new forms of media and business, is better suited to the more advanced student.

Wizard: The Comics Magazine. New York: Congers, 1991– . http://www.wizarduniverse.com.

Dedicated to the latest best sellers, *Wizard* is a monthly magazine designed to appeal to fans, collectors, and those who approach comics from a pop culture sensibility, in contrast to *The Comics Journal*'s arts sensibility. As such, it devotes most of its content to the top sellers in the industry and effects an irreverent editorial voice. A standard issue might contain interviews with the writers or artists of that month's most hotly anticipated comic book, a retrospective on a much-loved series from the recent past, a humorous article imagining popular characters in bizarre situations, or a visit to the set of the latest superhero movie. A great way to keep your eye on what is considered "hot" by comics fans.

Section 6: Publishers

There are hundreds of comic book and graphic novel publishers in the United States alone, ranging from small, single-person "self-publishers" who produce a book per year to massive media corporations that distribute dozens or even hundreds. It is beyond the scope of this book to provide a comprehensive look at them all. We have, instead, compiled a summary of some of the most important or recognizable companies.

Each listing summarizes basic company information and, where applicable, lists its Web site for further information. In general a publisher's Web site will contain a bit about the company's history and mission, listings of its titles, biographical information on the creators who have worked for it, and previews of upcoming titles. We point out exceptional features, especially those of particular interest to school librarians and/or newcomers to graphic novels.

ADV Manga

http://www.adv-manga.com

A division of AD Vision (an importer of Japanese anime), ADV Manga specializes in a diverse line of manga, many of which are adaptations of top-rated anime or have themselves been adapted into anime. From humor to science-fiction to romantic comedy and beyond, ADV Manga has an enormous library of titles. Its Web site features descriptions of each series, down to individual synopses for each volume.

Alternative Comics

http://www.indyworld.com/altcomics/

The self-styled "publisher of cool comics," including one of the works you read about in Chapter 3, Sara Varon's *Sweaterweather*.

Archie Comics

http://www.archiecomics.com

Publisher of the ever-popular (and ever-teenaged!) Archie and his gang of regulars: Betty, Veronica, Reggie, and more. The company's Web site is *extremely* child-friendly and child-oriented, with maps, contests, projects, and regular fun features for kids.

Cartoon Books

http://www.boneville.com

Cartoon Books publishes Allyson's students' favorite series, *Bone*. The site prides itself on being an open community for people who love Jeff Smith's opus. In addition to a cornucopia of fabulous pages related to *Bone*, the site also includes a "Library" section that promotes the work of other fine graphic novelists.

ComicsOne

http://www.comicsone.com

ComicsOne publishes cutting-edge manga and manhua (Chinese comics), including *Crouching Tiger, Hidden Dragon* (the series on which the Academy Award-winning movie was based) and, of course, the hilarious *Crayon ShinChan* (discussed in Chapter 3). The company's Web site contains a treasure trove for those looking to sample its wares: a plethora of samples of its titles, free for download in the PDF format.

CPM Manga

http://www.centralparkmedia.com/cpmcomics/index.cfm

CPM Manga is the manga publishing division of Central Park Media, a company known since 1990 for importing anime to the United States and helping to feed the ever-growing American hunger for Japanese storytelling. Since 1994 CPM Manga has imported top-selling manga titles such as *Alien Nine*, *Record of Lodoss War*, and *Geobreeders*, representing work by some of the top Japanese creators in comics.

CrossGen Comics

http://www.crossgen.com

CrossGen publishes an array of titles, from a roster of sci-fi/fantasy inspired titles to historical pirate epics and spy thrillers. Its title *Meridian* (discussed in Chapter 3) is particularly good for introducing girls to the thrills and fun of science fiction and fantasy.

Through its "Bridges" program (available for perusal on its Web site), CrossGen provides instructor guides and other materials for teachers to use, including worksheets and CD-ROMs. This makes the publisher and its titles very school-friendly, especially for those just beginning to incorporate graphic novels beyond recreational reading and into actual instruction.

Dark Horse Comics

http://libraries.darkhorse.com

Dark Horse Comics publishes a wide lineup of distinct titles, as evidenced in Chapter 3. The publisher's catalog includes such diverse fare as *Sock Monkey, Usagi Yojimbo, 300, Oh My Goddess!, What's Michael?*, and *Concrete*. (By the time you read this book, the publisher's roster will also include *Castle Waiting*, previously published by Olio Press.)

Bearing in mind the special needs of librarians, Dark Horse created this Web site, specifically devoted to librarians. The site includes information about current titles, information about upcoming titles, reviews of Dark Horse graphic novels, and a list of best sellers. To access the site's features, you'll need to create a log-in name and password for yourself, but Dark Horse does not use this information to spam you, only to limit access to this area to the people who truly can use it.

DC Comics

http://www.dccomics.com

DC Comics is best known around the world as the publisher of some of history's most popular comic book characters, names that have practically become synonymous with the comic book medium; Batman, Superman, Green Lantern, Aquaman, The Flash, and Wonder Woman are only the beginning. DC also maintains imprints that publish titles other than superhero fare. Vertigo is an imprint designed for mature readers and has spawned such classics as *Sandman* and *Y, The Last Man*, among others. Paradox Press is devoted to titles that are more at home in a standard book environment, such as the *Big Book* series and *Road to Perdition* (the crime thriller graphic novel that became an Academy Award-winning movie). The Wildstorm imprint features books with cutting-edge superheroes, written with an older reader in mind.

Devil's Due

http://www.devilsdue.net/

Devil's Due publishes an eclectic blend of titles, including the sci-fi fantasy *Misplaced* (a sort of futuristic *Alice in Wonderland* in reverse). The company is perhaps best known, though, for its line of comics based on some of the most popular licenses in pop culture: *G.I. Joe, Micronauts, Voltron, Dragonlance*, and George R. R. Martin's *A Song of Fire and Ice*. Many of these properties are already familiar to your students from toys, movies, and television, making them highly likely to read the comics. (In the case of Martin's work, reading the comics could very well get reluctant readers interested enough to pick up the novels themselves.)

Doubleday/Random House Graphic Novels

http://www.randomhouse.com/doubleday/graphicnovels/

The official Web site for Doubleday/Random House's graphics novel line, which includes such titles as *Shutterbug Follies, Narcissa*, and *Fagin the Jew*, Will Eisner's retelling of *Oliver Twist* from a different perspective.

Drawn & Quarterly

http://www.drawnandquarterly.com

A literary comics publisher that has published work by such luminaries as Adrian Tomine, Seth, Chester Brown, Joe Matt, Julie Doucet, James Sturm, and Debbie Drechsler (including Drechsler's *Summer of Love*, covered in Chapter 3).

Dreamwave

http://www.dreamwaveprod.com

Dreamwave publishes comics based on the highly popular *Transformers*, of movie, toy, and television fame. Another property that your students are already familiar with and will be drawn to.

Fantagraphics Books

http://www.fantagraphics.com

Fantagraphics is a venerable publisher of art and literary comics, focused on producing work of enduring value and beauty that compares favorably with the best art of other fields of endeavor. The company's Web site features archives, galleries, and biographical information on its creators, as well as information on upcoming projects, including a true American treasure: a series collecting the complete run of Charles Schulz's *Peanuts* for the first time in history. (Note that Fantagraphics publishes adult comics through a subsidiary named Eros, which is linked from its main site.) Fantagraphics is also the publisher of *The Comics Journal*.

Gemstone Publishing

http://www.gemstonepub.com/Disney

Gemstone Publishing has exclusive rights to publish Disney comics, meaning that this is the place to visit for information on *Uncle Scrooge, Walt Disney's Comics and Stories, Donald Duck Adventures, Donald Duck and Friends,* and *Mickey Mouse and Friends.* Gemstone also publishes *The Overstreet Comic Book Price Guide* (see above).

Image Comics

http://www.imagecomics.com

Formed in 1992 by a group of top creators who left Marvel Comics to form their own publishing company, Image hosts a variety of creators and properties. Image acts as a sort of "central clearinghouse" for associated creators and studios, giving them a common "umbrella" under which to publish. As a result, its publishing list is quite diverse, including everything from superheroes to crime fiction to thrillers to slice-of-life tales to Eric Shanower's award-winning adaptation of the Trojan War, *Age of Bronze* (discussed in Chapter 3). Its Web site allows you to browse over a hundred titles by studio or genre.

In addition to its array of titles from independent creators and studios, Image also publishes books from the studios formed by many of its original founders: Top Cow Productions publishes titles such as *Witchblade* and *Tomb Raider* (based on the video game and movie character), while Todd McFarlane Productions publishes the popular Spawn and related comics. Original founder Erik Larsen continues to publish his superhero comic *Savage Dragon* through Image as well.

Marvel Comics

http://www.marvel.com

Marvel Comics is best known for its plethora of world-famous superheroes, including names that your students will already know from years of movies, cartoons, and video games: Spider-Man, The Hulk, The X-Men, the Fantastic Four, and more. The company's Web site includes Marvel's "dotComics," a program that provides free comic book samples online for anyone to read. Marvel also publishes a line for mature readers under its "MAX" imprint.

MV Creations

http://www.mvcreations.com

Among its many titles, MV Creations includes *Masters of the Universe*, based on the TV series and toy line. Your students already know the characters (and their parents probably remember them from the 1980s!), so this is a great way to get reluctant readers to try reading something.

NBM Publishing

http://www.nbmpub.com

NBM organizes its graphic novels into the following categories: Classic Tales, ComicsLit, Eurotica, Fantasy/SF/Horror, Humor, Mystery, and Reference. (We doubt you'll have any use for the adult-oriented Eurotica titles in a school setting, but remember that this site is meant for the general public.) NBM has included a helpful link "For Libraries," which has review information for the publishers' titles that come highly recommended by any combination of the following: *Library Journal*, *Booklist*, *Kirkus Reviews*, *Publishers Weekly*, and *School Library Journal*. In Chapter 3 you saw a sampling of NBM's titles: *Li'l Santa*, *The Yellow Jar*, *Moby Dick*, and *Sundiata*.

Oni Press

http://www.onipress.com

From the political spy thriller *Queen & Country* to the superhero hilarity of *Madman* to the foul-mouthed (but addictive) comedy *Barry Ween*, Oni Press publishes top-notch graphic novels from creators at the top of their games. Its list runs from mature readers fare to child-friendly titles such as *Alison Dare*, which we discussed in Chapter 3. The company's Web site features free downloadable comics for your review, as well as free AOL Instant Messenger icons of some of its most popular characters.

Pantheon/Random House Graphic Novels

http://www.randomhouse.com/pantheon/graphicnovels/

Pantheon publishes both graphic novels and books about graphic novels, including retrospectives on creators as diverse as Charles Schulz and Alex Ross. Biographical information about Alex Ross, Marjane Satrapi, Kim Deitch, Sarah Boxer, Raymond Briggs, Daniel Clowes, Charles Schulz, Matt Groening, Ben Katchor, Art Spiegelman, and Chris Ware can be found here, making this site a resource not only for teachers but also for students.

Renaissance Press

Renaissance Press publishes Jimmy Gownley's *Amelia Rules* (discussed in Chapter 3) in its serialized comic book form. The graphic novels are collected and published by iBooks.

Slave Labor Graphics

http://www.slavelabor.com

Founded in 1986, Slave Labor Graphics publishes a number of acclaimed graphic novels, including *Lenore*, *Trashed*, *Waiting Place*, *Gloom Cookie*, and *Squee*. In 1995, SLG launched its Amaze Ink imprint, which publishes all-ages, genre-oriented titles such as *Skeleton Key* and *Sleeping Dragons*.

TokyoPop

http://www.tokyopop.com

TokyoPop is one of the largest importers of manga in the United States, with hundreds of titles in its backlist and more shipping every month. Subjects run the gamut from horror to comedy and everything in between, with all age groups represented. The company Web site provides an introduction, creator profile, and character information for each series, as well as descriptions of each volume in the series.

Top Shelf Productions

http://www.topshelfcomix.com

Publisher of fine art comics, Top Shelf produces titles covered in Chapter 3 such as James Kochalka's *Pinky & Stinky* and *Monkey vs. Robot*, and *three fingers*. Top Shelf has also gained attention and critical acclaim for many other titles, including *Good-bye, Chunky Rice* and *Blankets*. Its Web site maintains a complete listing of titles, as well as creator biographies, an archive of interviews, and more.

TwoMorrows

http://www.twomorrows.com

TwoMorrows is dedicated to preserving the history of comics through a line of books and magazines that examine and critique specific titles, characters, and creators. The publisher is known for volumes that take in-depth looks at individual subjects, complete with interviews, reprints of crucial and important work, and the publication of "lost" work that has never been published. TwoMorrows also publishes titles dedicated to explaining the creative process behind comics, from writing instruction to art lessons. An excellent source of material on comics history and instruction for budding comic book creators.

Viz Communications, Inc.

http://www.viz.com

Founded in 1986, Viz is one of the leading importers of Japanese storytelling into the United States, with an impressive list of anime and manga in its catalog. The Web site contains a list of "online manga," which are readable graphic novel stories presented in formats acceptable for low- and high-bandwidth connections. You can also download a donation request form, as Viz sometimes provides free copies of its titles to certain institutions (including libraries) that meet its criteria. Viz publishes the wildly popular *Ranma ½* series, discussed in Chapter 3.

Section 7: Reviews of Graphic Novels/Comic Books

Reliable sources for reviews of graphic novels are not difficult to find. As we mentioned before, many Web sites and publications devoted to comics review them regularly, but not with an eye toward the needs of librarians. Below is a list of print and online sources for reviews that meet the needs of school librarians.

Artbomb.net: A Graphic Novel Explosion

http://www.artbomb.net

Under the auspices of award-winning graphic novelist Warren Ellis and author Peter Siegel, Artbomb has become an authoritative Web site on the world of graphic novels. The site features reviews on current graphic novels, searchable by either genre or creator. One of the site's gems is free online graphic novels. Another perk is a terrific bonus for novices: an Introduction section that walks you through a graphic novel, literally, within two pages of a comic. The Introduction section would be well suited for a staff development on graphic novels as well as a workshop for students and parents.

Booklist

http://www.ala.org

A publication of the American Library Association, *Booklist* is a monthly magazine devoted to reviewing books and electronic media for librarians. It has recently begun adding regular graphic novel reviews to the thousands of titles it reviews each year.

The Diamond Bookshelf

http://bookshelf.diamondcomics.com

As mentioned in the discussion of Diamond Comic Distributors, The Diamond Bookshelf features monthly reviews from librarian Kat Kan, who also writes reviews for *VOYA*. On the Bookshelf, Kat focuses mainly on reviews for titles aimed at children and adults.

No Flying, No Tights

http://www.noflyingnotights.com

Robin Brenner's site is a cornucopia of information about graphic novels, broken down by genre and interest level. (Brenner is a library technician at Cary Memorial Library in Lexington, Massachusetts.) For the younger reader, her Web page "Sidekicks for Kids" includes an annotated list of graphic novel titles suitable for children. For the teens, she lists a comprehensive collection of titles based on genre and reading interest level. Finally, for older teens and adults, there is "The Lair," with reviews of graphic novels that have more adult content. This site is made appealing by virtue of being current, trendy, and humorous. Your students who read comics probably already know about this site, so check it out to bring in the best graphic novels to your collection and have an inking as to what your students are talking about!

Publishers Weekly

http://www.publishersweekly.com

Publishers Weekly now runs regular coverage of the comic book industry (particularly of graphic novels and how they pertain to book markets) and runs a special review section on graphic novels on a quarterly basis.

School Library Journal

http://www.schoollibraryjournal.com/

Aimed at school librarians, *School Library Journal* contains its "Graphic Novel Roundup" of graphic novel reviews on a bimonthly basis.

VOYA: Voice of Youth Advocates

http://www.voya.com

A bimonthly magazine dedicated to librarians who deal with young adults. Each issue features "Graphically Speaking," a column by librarian Kat Kan that reviews YA-appropriate graphic novels.

Section 8: Wonderful Web Sites for Reference and Teaching

One of the best parts about being a media specialist, librarian, or (for our Canadian friends) teacher librarian is the opportunity to collaborate with teachers. Here are some great Web sites to use in lessons, especially with art teachers. Plan a unit with a teacher using these Web sites for assistance. Have fun!

The Comic Book Periodic Table of the Elements

http://www.uky.edu/Projects/Chemcomics/

This site is definitely not for serious use but is very entertaining and can be used to teach actual science, after a fashion. It offers an interactive periodic table of elements; select an element and its use in a comic book will be displayed. Most times, the element is used incorrectly, but often it isn't, and lessons can be built around comparing the real use of a particular element with its comic book use. This is a fun and quirky site—share it with your chemistry teachers!

Museum of Comic and Cartoon Art

http://www.moccany.org

Most educators probably do not know of this museum's existence, so please take a look at this Web site, which is a small, virtual glimpse into the real thing. The mission of the Museum of Comic and Cartoon Art is to "educate the public about comic and cartoon art, how it is crafted, and how it reflects history. What does the art tell us about the time period that it was created in? How does it stand the test of time? What First Amendment issues regarding content come into play? How does censorship determine what is (and isn't) published?"

If you cannot visit the museum in person, the Web site has links to art, photographs, and museum events. Since the museum is dedicated to education, it sponsors workshops for children, art shows, and even classes for credit at New York University.

The New York City Comic Book Museum

http://www.nyccomicbookmuseum.org/education/education.htm

One of the coolest Web sites around for one of the most unique museums in New York City. Great reference information for students doing research on comic books and their art form, and a terrific idea for a field trip.

Section 9: Conventions

For the complete comic book experience, you really should attend a comic book convention at least once in your life. Comic book conventions, like conventions of all kinds, attract fans from all around the world. It's an opportunity for people with a shared love of comics to meet; mingle; shop for hard-to-find items; and meet the publishers, writers, and artists who tell the stories that thrill them. It's also a great opportunity for those same creators to meet the people who enjoy their work! This sort of closeness between creators and fans is one of the hallmarks of the comic book industry and has been a constant for much of its history.

A comic book convention will bring out all types: the professional who loves old comics and is looking for that elusive issue, the teenager who's looking for the next big thing, the true-blue fan who dresses up as his or her favorite character, and, of course, folks who are just interested in comics and all they have to offer.

There are hundreds (if not thousands) of conventions of all sizes and types around the United States each year. We've tried to list some of the biggest, the ones where you'll have the best chance of seeing the most. We've also tried to hit all the major geographical areas to make it easy for everyone to try a "con" at least once.

Baltimore Comic-Con

http://www.comicon.com/Baltimore/

Held in mid-September, the Baltimore Comic-Con is a relatively new show that has built its reputation by focusing on comic books and their creators, almost to the exclusion of ancillary and related products (such as toys and videos) and the celebrity guests that other shows use. The result is a show purely dedicated to comics and nothing else. The organizers plan special school activities and give discounts to students and teachers who show school ID.

Comic-Con International: San Diego

http://www.comic-con.org

Held each year in July, Comic-Con International: San Diego (known in the industry simply as "San Diego") is the single largest comic book event of the year. Publishers big and small, entire armies of talent, and tens of thousands of fans descend on San Diego each year for the unparalleled experience of seeing everyone who's anyone in comics under one (huge!) roof. In recent years, the show has become an enormous multimedia extravaganza, with representatives from every kind of entertainment available: Toy makers, movie studios, and others set up booths side-by-side with the comic book industry, making for an astonishing array of sights and sounds. It must be seen to be believed.

HeroesCon

http://www.heroesonline.com/con-update.htm

Organized by Shelton Drum, proprietor of respected comic book store Heroes Aren't Hard to Find, HeroesCon is a staple of the industry and is strongly dedicated to bringing top talents into contact with fans. The show is held in Charlotte, North Carolina, each year, usually on or around Father's Day weekend.

MegaCon

http://www.megaconvention.com

In early March, Orlando, Florida, plays host to MegaCon, a comic book convention with celebrities mixed in for whole-family fun. Best of all, MegaCon's location makes it an ideal family vacation destination—the con itself is family-friendly, and it can easily be combined with a trip to Disney World or Universal Studios.

Mid-Ohio Con

http://www.midohiocon.com

For twenty-five years, Mid-Ohio Con has brought top-rated comic book creators to Columbus, Ohio, to meet and greet fans. Usually held in late November, the con is a perfect Thanksgiving weekend getaway.

Wizard World

http://www.wizarduniverse.com/conventions/

Organized and run by the publisher of *Wizard* magazine, the Wizard World conventions offer a festive atmosphere, large crowds, big and small publishers alike, and plenty of talent on-hand, including guests of honor that typically include Hollywood stars (such as Kevin Smith). There are multiple Wizard Worlds held throughout the year, though the largest is in Chicago:

Chicago (August)

Long Beach, California (March)

Arlington, Texas (November)

Philadelphia (late May)

WonderCon

http://www.comic-con.org

Held by the same organization that arranges San Diego, WonderCon is usually held in San Francisco in late April/early May of each year.

7

Lesson Plans

Thus far, you have been introduced to the graphic novel in terms of its history, composition, development, and utility. By now you understand what graphic novels are, how they come to be, why they are useful to you in the school media environment, and how to justify their usage. You may be wondering exactly *how* to use them, though, short of simply adding them to your collection!

In this chapter we present lesson plans for a range of grade levels, using titles discussed in Chapter 3. Use these lesson plans as a jumping-off point for your own development of lessons that revolve around graphic novels, and start to explore how much good these titles can do for your students. (Some of the lesson plans are designed for use outside the media center—a great way to get colleagues interested in your new collection, and a terrific opportunity to encourage collaboration!)

Lesson Plan 1: *Li'l Santa* by Thierry Robin and Lewis Trondheim

Unit/Curricular Connections: Holidays, Christmas, language arts—sequencing of story, wordless books, dialogue between characters, creative writing

Grade Level: Elementary, grades 2–5, may be completed with kindergarten and first grades as a class activity

Objective: By the end of the lesson, students will create original dialogue for the characters and panels of *Li'l Santa.*

Direct Teaching: Share the entire book with the class. Depending on the length of the class, it may take two twenty-minute sessions to complete the sharing and discussion of the book. Since this is a wordless book, discuss what is happening in each panel with the students. Focus the students' attention on the facial expressions of the characters, the action in the panels, and the use of lines and shading to suggest movement and action.

Writing Activity: After sharing the book, students will separate into small groups to write original dialogue for the story. Depending on the size of the class, pairs, trios, or quads may be utilized. As an educator, you may copy each page in the book once for teaching purposes. (The pages in *Li'l Santa* are not numbered, so the copies that are made will need to be numbered.) In addition, with a small pen, number the panels so that the students can write their original dialogue to correspond to the numbered panel on the page. So that the pages may be used with different classes, laminate the pages for longevity. Give each group a page in the story and the corresponding worksheet (more than one sheet might be needed) and create a master list of which group has which page number. Give the students two class periods to write their original dialogue and narrative for their assigned page of the book. After the students have completed their writing, reread the story, but this time allowing the students to read their dialogue with the corresponding page.

Technology Connection: Students may use Kid Pix to create an original wordless holiday story. These may be tied together to create a slide show.

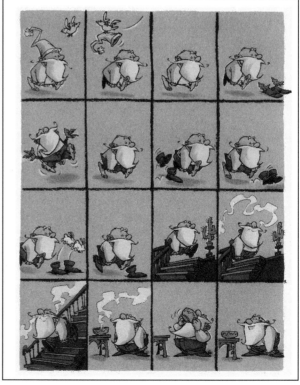

Figures 7.1. and 7.2. © 2000 Dupuis & © 2002 NBM. Two sample pages from *Li'l Santa*. Completely wordless, they nevertheless tell a story, with characterization, action, plot development, and mood all created without dialogue. Now imagine the fun your students will have supplying their own dialogue, while learning how to construct and decode story meaning at the same time.

Li'l Santa Story Sheet

Name: _____

Teacher's Name: _____

Panel Number: _____

Dialogue:

_____

_____

_____

_____

_____

_____

_____

_____

_____

Panel Number: _____

Dialogue:

_____

_____

_____

_____

_____

_____

_____

_____

_____

Panel Number: _____

Dialogue:

_____

_____

_____

_____

_____

_____

_____

_____

_____

Lesson Plan 2: *The Wolves in the Walls* by Neil Gaiman and Dave McKean

Unit/Curricular Connections: Media, visual literacy

Grade Level: Elementary, grades 4 and 5

Objective: Students will analyze the following:

a. how the font sizes, font type, and position of the words on the page influence the mood and convey the story, and

b. the use of photographs in the story opposed to all illustrations.

Direct Teaching: To become acquainted with this graphic novel story, take a picture walk with the students without reading the text of the story. Point out and lead a discussion of the use of panels, different font sizes, and photographs in the book.

Activity: For the second lesson, read the book aloud to the students. As the students are hearing and visually reading the story, they will take notes on the elements of font, word placement, illustrations, and photographs on their worksheet. Allow thirty seconds between pages so students can take notes on what they have observed. After the story is finished, a class discussion can proceed based on the notes that the students took on the story.

Reflection Question/Writing Prompt: How does the artist's style and choice of font and illustrations influence and/or communicate the story and mood of the book? How might different choices in these areas change the book?

Technology Connection: Using a drawing program like Kid Pix or other software, assign a pair of students a page from *Wolves from the Walls*. With the software, they must recreate the page but with modifications to the font style, word placement, and sizing to alter the feeling and mood of the original story.

The Wolves in the Walls

Student's Name: _____

Teacher's Name: _____

What are you seeing on the pages? Please take notes on these traits as the story is being read to you.

Font size, style, and shape	Placement of words on page
Illustrations: Type, style, line, movement	**Other notes and observations**

Lesson Plan 3: *Monkey vs. Robot* by James Kochalka

Unit/Curricular Connections: Language arts—humans versus nature in literature, environmental science/ social studies, impact of technology on environment/rain forests

Grade Level: Elementary, grades 3–5

Objective: Students will determine the impact technology and humans have on the environment, particularly animal habitats.

Direct Teaching: Share the story *Monkey vs. Robot* with the class. Since this is a lengthy book, two class periods should be utilized. *Monkey vs. Robot* is a graphic novel with few words, so an appropriate class discussion should take place during the reading of the book to analyze the content of the story as the class is sharing it.

Activity: After reading the book, students will complete a cause-and-effect chart based on the incidents in the book. Students will analyze the impact the robot/technology had on the life and habitat of the monkey. After completing the chart, lead a class discussion based on the students' answers and compile a class chart on the overhead.

Reflection Questions: Based on what you learned about the effects technology has on the environment, how do you think technology could change to help the environment? What new inventions do you think would be more helpful to humans and the environment? What can be done to save animal habitats instead of destroying them?

Technology Connection: Students may use the Internet to research special interest groups that are working to save rain forests and animal habitats, and also to collect data on the damage to the environment caused by technology and human interference (land development, tourism, deforestation, etc.). After the research has been conducted, students may create a PowerPoint presentation to share their knowledge.

Monkey vs. Robot: Cause and Effect

Student's Name: _____

Teacher's Name: _____

    In the graphic novel *Monkey vs. Robot*, there were many instances in which the Monkey's habitat was disrupted by the Robot. In the chart below, please list the causes of environmental destruction and their effects.

Cause	Effect

Lesson Plan 4: *Sundiata: A Legend of Africa* (retold by Will Eisner)

Unit/Curricular Connections: Social studies, African history, Africa, ancient African rulers, character education, visual literacy

Grade Level: Upper elementary/middle school

Objective: Students will learn about Sundiata, the ruler of ancient Mali, and compare and contrast the graphic novel *Sundiata* to other books about Sundiata.

Direct Teaching: Introduce the ruler Sundiata and the three books to the students: *Sundiata* by Will Eisner, *Sundiata: Lion King of Mali* by David Wisniewski, and *Sundiata: An Epic of Old Mali, Longman African Writers Series,* by D. T. Niane. If you are working with middle school students, the students can read the books independently. If you are working with upper elementary students, those reading at or above grade level can work independently, while the others can work in a small group with you or as a whole-class group lesson. Establish in class discussion that each of these books covers the same content, the ruler Sundiata. However, each book has a different presentation of the information: a picture book, a graphic novel, and a text. Inform the students that they are responsible for reading and analyzing all three and completing the graphic organizer about the books.

Activity: Students will read the three books and complete the graphic organizer on paper or use Kidspiration or Inspiration to create their own graphic organizers to compare and contrast the three books.

Writing Prompt: Based on your analysis of the three books about Sundiata, which one best communicates the story of his life? Be sure to cite examples from the book you have chosen to support your argument.

Technology Connection: There are many wonderful Web sites with curricular connections to *Sundiata.* They contain lesson plans, historical information, maps, and biographical information on Sundiata the ruler:

Core Values Internet Resource Library Sub-Saharan Africa Curriculum : Unit 2 Sub-Saharan Africa: Lesson Plans & Curriculum Guides: http://tlc.ousd.k12.ca.us/library/africa/africa_lessons.html

History of Mali: http://www.princetonol.com/groups/iad/lessons/middle/histmali.htm

Virginia Museum of Fine Arts: Mali Lesson Plans: (http://mali.pwnet.org/lessonplan/lessonplan_fine_art.htm)

Sundiata: Ruler of Mali

Will the real Sundiata stand up and be read?

Student's Name: _____

Teacher's Name: _____

Complete the graphic organizer below to make a final choice about which book best tells the story of Sundiata.

CATEGORY	AUTHOR		
	Eisner	Wisniewski	Niane
Facts			
Visual appeal			
Relationship between text and pictures			
Readability			
Clarity of writing (How easy is the story to understand?)			

Lesson Plan 5: *Moby Dick* by Herman Melville (adapted by Will Eisner)

Unit/Curricular Connections: Literature, Herman Melville

Grade Level: High school

Objective: Students will read *Moby Dick* to analyze the conflicts of humanity versus nature and humanity versus itself. Students will also learn about whaling in nineteenth-century America.

Direct Teaching: Using Inspiration software or a graphic organizer on the computer or overhead, students will brainstorm their knowledge of the whaling trade in nineteenth-century America and the hardships involved. List all the facts that the students give, regardless of whether or not the information is correct. If the students have little prior knowledge about whaling, have them conduct research on the topic of the whaling industry in New England in the early 1800s. After the research is finished, go back to the original brainstormed list to check the facts for accuracy. Make corrections and additions as needed.

Reflection Questions: Have the students read the book in pairs. As they are reading the story or after they have read the story, have them answer the reflection questions. Share the answers as a class for a meaningful discussion on the book.

1. What do you think is the significance of Moby Dick's color?

2. *Moby Dick* was first published as a novel. How does the graphic novel adaptation of this story help you to understand the story? What parts of the story do you think would be difficult to understand if you were reading the text version?

3. In his quest for the great white whale, Ahab is consumed with the desire to conquer. Do you think he is passionate to conquer Moby Dick or something else, or a combination?

4. Do you think Melville made an environmental statement in his book? Why or why not? State examples from the book to support your answer.

Technology Connection: Here are three Web sites that are useful for general knowledge about Herman Melville and whales:

The Life and Works of Herman Melville: http://www.melville.org/

Whales in Literature: http://www.keele.ac.uk/depts/as/Literature/Moby-Dick/amlit.whale-pages.html

Whale-Watching-Web: http://www.physics.helsinki.fi/whale/

Research Organizer for Nineteenth-Century Whaling

Student's Name: _____

Class: _____

Describe what you believe to be the living conditions on a nineteenth-century whaling ship. How can you defend this position? Give facts, research, data, etc.

Who do you think sought jobs in whaling? Why? Think of factors such as age, education, gender, race, and social class.

List what facts you know about whales in the nineteenth century, including number of whales in the world, migration routes, uses for whales, etc.

Lesson Plan 6: *The Yellow Jar* by Patrick Atangan

Unit/Curricular Connections: Japanese folk tales, Japanese ukiyo-e, art history

Grade Level: Middle school and high school art and art history, middle school and high school literature

Objectives: By the end of the lesson, students will have read *The Yellow Jar* and *Two Chrysanthemum Maidens* and identified the importance of nature in Japanese folk tales. Also by the end of the lesson, students will identify traits of Japanese ukiyo-e (Japanese for "floating images," a particular type of artwork) and create a ukiyo-e print of their own.

Direct Teaching: *The Yellow Jar* contains two tales: *The Yellow Jar* and *Two Chrysanthemum Maidens*. Read and examine each story separately. Depending on the length of the class, this may take two twenty-minute sessions to complete the sharing and discussion of the book. While the students are reading the stories, they may complete an organizer to guide them in their thinking about nature's role in the story. After completing the reading and organizer, discuss the book as a class and identify key points in which nature played a role in the stories.

For the art objective, the book can be read and studied entirely as a class or in pairs. Since the art is very detailed, discuss what is happening in each panel with the students. Focus the students' attention on the facial expressions of the characters, the action in the panels, and the use of lines and shading to suggest movement and action. The art also represents Japanese culture, so have the students take note of clothing, architecture, and landscape.

Art Activity: After sharing the book, students will create their own ukiyo-e prints, emulating the style and colors of Hiroshige's ukiyo-e prints or Atangan's style of ukiyo-e prints.

Technology Connection: Explore more Japanese ukiyo-e by visiting the following sites with your students. Compare and contrast the content and style of the art with the art found in *The Yellow Jar.*

Ukiyo-E: The Pictures of the Floating World: http://www.bahnhof.se/~secutor/ukiyo-e/

The Japan Ukiyo-E Museum: http://www.cjn.or.jp/ukiyo-e/

Ukiyoe-Gallery: http://www.ukiyoe-gallery.com/

The Yellow Jar

Student's Name: _____

Date: _____

Class: _____

The Yellow Jar

Interaction/Presence of Nature	Meaning

Two Chrysanthemum Maidens

Interaction/Presence of Nature	Meaning

Lesson Plan 7: *Age of Bronze:* *A Thousand Ships* by Eric Shanower

Note: This is actually a unit plan, as *Age of Bronze* is an incredibly rich, dense source for your class. Like any good novel or extended work, it lends itself to being taught over a long period of time, with many lessons. This is a suggested guide for doing so.

Unit/Curricular Connections: Greek studies and literature, Trojan War

Grade Level: High school

Objective: By the end of the unit, students will have learned about the Greek empire and the Trojan War, particularly the importance of Troy.

Direct Teaching: This book can be used for an entire semester of Greek studies. The book contains a rich bibliography, glossary of names, and genealogical charts, and an afterword in which the author explains his motivations for telling this story in this fashion. Have the students read the afterword first and then begin reading the book. During the reading of the book, have the students consult the glossary of names and genealogical charts for comprehension of the relationships between the characters. Since class times vary, determine starting and stopping points for class reading and discussion. To further illustrate the tension and stress leading to war, separate the class into two sides: the Trojan Royal Family and the Achaeans. Each side should represent the people and their viewpoints on the war.

Extension: After reading *Age of Bronze: A Thousand Ships,* have the students read Homer's *Iliad* and *Odyssey* and compare and contrast the stories.

Lesson Plan 8: *Pinky & Stinky*
by James Kochalka

Unit/Curricular Connections: Reading, literature, literary traits

Grade Level: Elementary, grades 3–5

Objective: By the end of the lesson, students will understand: character traits, onomatopoeia, and conflict between characters.

Direct Teaching: Share the entire book with the class. Depending on the length of the class, it may take two thirty-minute sessions to complete the sharing and discussion of the book. Or, have pairs of students read the book independently and answer the reflection questions. Afterward, have the students share their answers to the questions in oral discussion.

Questions for Discussion and/or Written Reflection:

1. What are Templeton's uncle's feelings toward the space program?

2. How is the literary element onomatopoeia used in this story?

3. What character traits does Stinky the Pig exhibit when he is attempting to rescue Pinky and himself from the crash?

4. Why do you think the astronauts treat the piggies so poorly?

5. What actions of the astronauts make them think they are better than (superior to) the Ice People and the piggies?

6. Why do you suppose the human astronauts have a conflict with the Ice People?

7. How are the piggies rewarded at the end of the story?

8. What did the piggies gain by befriending the Ice Princess?

Technology Connection: Students may use Kid Pix to create an original Pinky & Stinky story of their own.

Lesson Plan 9: *Crayon ShinChan* by Yoshito Usui

Unit/Curricular Connections: Literature, manga-Japanese graphic novels, Japanese culture

Grade Level: Grades 8–12

Objective: By the end of the lesson, students will compare and contrast American and Japanese culture by observing differences between gender, rituals, clothing, shelter, and food.

Direct Teaching: Since this book has chapters, assign reading chapters based on the length of the class period. This book can be read as a class (with lots of laughing out loud) or in pairs. While reading the story, students can complete the cultural differences/similarities organizer. Direct oral discussion of the book can take place by using the chart to generate discussion of the book.

Crayon ShinChan: Cultural Differences

Student's Name: _____

Date: _____

Class: _____

While reading the story, identify differences between the two cultures.

Cultural Traits	Japanese	American
Gender roles		
Rituals (shopping, bathing)		
Clothing		
Food		
Shelter/furniture		
Private behavior		
Public behavior		

Crayon ShinChan: Cultural Similarities

Student's Name: _____
Date: _____
Class: _____

While reading the story, identify similarities between the two cultures.

Cultural Traits	Japanese	American
Gender roles		
Rituals (shopping, bathing)		
Clothing		
Food		
Shelter/furniture		
Private behavior		
Public behavior		

Lesson Plan 10: *Amelia Rules*
by Jimmy Gownley

Unit/Curricular Connections: Guidance—feelings with divorce

Grade Level: Elementary and middle school

Objective: Students will read this book to explore their own emotions with regard to divorce and use Amelia's reactions to problems to enhance their own problem-solving skills.

Direct Teaching: Purchase multiple copies of this book so that students can have their own copies or share a copy with a partner. Depending on the grade level, students can take turns reading the pages so that a chapter is has been read at the end of the session.

Reflection Questions:

1. How does Amelia deal with moving to a new town?

2. What steps does Amelia take to make new friends?

3. How does Amelia express her feelings about her parents' divorce?

4. Who does Amelia trust the most with her feelings? Who do you trust the most to share your feelings with?

5. What role does Aunt Tanner play in Amelia's life? Do you have someone like Aunt Tanner in your life?

6. How does humor help Amelia?

7. What are some things that Amelia does to stay busy? What can you do to stay busy?

8. Amelia gets in trouble in school a lot. Why do you think she is having problems? What can she do to be more successful in school?

9. Sometimes Amelia hears her parents arguing on the phone. Does this happen to you? What can you do to feel better? Who can you talk to?

10. Amelia learns to talk openly with her father. How did this help their relationship? What can you do to improve your relationship with your parents?

The following seven lesson plans will take you through the entire graphic novel *Castle Waiting*: *The Lucky Road* by Linda Medley. Each chapter has its own lesson plan.

Lesson Plan 11: *Castle Waiting: The Lucky Road* by Linda Medley
Chapter 1—"Bahtalo Drom"

Unit/Curricular Connection: Folk and fairy tales, medieval times/literature

Grade Level: Grades 4–6 and high school for comparative literature

Objective: By the end of the lesson, students will be introduced to the vocabulary of the story and its characters.

Direct Teaching:

1. Introduce the vocabulary of the story:

    "rom" = gypsy

    "chavo" = boy

    "rahnie" = great lady

    "gorgio" = non-gypsy

    "graiengeri" = horsetrader

    "bahtalo drom" = "lucky road"

2. Reading of the story can be done independently, with partners, or as a whole class; you will have to decide based on grade level and reading ability. With younger students, it is recommended that the first chapter be read as a whole class until the students have mastered the format and language. Stop periodically during the story to check for comprehension. After reading the story, have the students complete the reflection questions.

Reflection Questions:

1. Based on the graphic novel, what type of relationship did Orson and Lady Jain have? What evidence do you have?

2. What do you think happened to Lady Jain to force her to leave her home?

3. The Three Little Pigs give Lady Jain advice when she leaves: "Don't talk to wolves" and "Don't take any wooden groshen." What other advice could the pigs give Lady Jain?

4. At what point in the story do we realize Lady Jain is pregnant?

5. Nubbin Sully is unable to cut the bag away from Lady Jain. What circumstances would prevent him from doing so?

6. What made Lady Jain realize that Dido and Nubbin Sully were out to rob her?

Activity: Jain's father made a map to record his travels. He used symbols to mark each place that he visited. Some symbols mean "good for trade," "bad roads," or "tourist trap." Have the students make their own map of places that they have visited and create a legend and symbols for their map. Have each symbol mean a different thing, for example, "good restaurant," "skateboarding park," or "snowball stand."

Lesson Plan 12: *Castle Waiting: The Lucky Road* by Linda Medley

Chapter 2—"Your Castle Is Your Home"

Unit/Curricular Connection: Folk and fairy tales, medieval times/literature

Grade Level: Grades 4–6 and high school for comparative literature

Objective: By the end of the lesson, students will know more about the setting of the story and be introduced to new characters.

Direct Teaching:

1. Review the characters and plot from "Bahtalo Drom."

2. Define vocabulary terms: *loquacious, sanctuary.*

3. Reading of the story can be done independently, with partners, or as a whole class; you will have to decide based on grade level and reading ability. Stop periodically during the story to check for comprehension. After reading the story, have the students complete the reflection questions.

Reflection Questions:

1. Lady Jain hopes to find sanctuary at Castle Waiting. What does this mean? Why do you suppose she needs sanctuary?

2. Henry was "called." In terms of his personality, what does this mean?

3. There are many different types of people at Castle Waiting. What does each character represent in society? Who do these characters remind you of in your own life, and why?

Activity: At the beginning of the story, Rackham Adjutant was telling about the history and building materials of Castle Waiting. Have the students research a famous castle and construct a replica.

Additional Resources:

Castle by Christopher Gravett (Penguin, 2002)

Castles by Philip Steele (Larousse Kingfisher Chambers, 1995)

Knights and Castles: 50 Hands-on Activities to Experience the Middle Ages by Avery Hart and Paul Mantell (Bt Bound, 2003)

Lesson Plan 13: *Castle Waiting: The Lucky Road* by Linda Medley

Chapter 3—"Labors of Love"

Unit/Curricular Connection: Folk and fairy tales, medieval times/literature

Grade Level: Grades 4–6 and high school for comparative literature

Objective: By the end of the lesson, students will know how important reading becomes for one character in the story.

Direct Teaching:

1. Review the characters and plot from "Your Castle Is Your Home."

2. Reading of the story can be done independently, with partners, or as a whole class; you will have to decide based on grade level and reading ability. Stop periodically during the story to check for comprehension. After reading the story, have the students complete the reflection questions.

Reflection Questions:

1. Based on what you have read, how does Rackham demonstrate his affection for Simon and for Lady Jain?

2. Why do you think Simon wants to read? How do you think this will change his character?

Activities:

1. Since Simon is learning to read and likes picture books, have the students create a new picture book for him to read that features him as the main character.

2. Dr. Fell was using medieval ways to figure out the sex of the baby. Have the students do some research about medieval medicine and share a written or visual report on their findings.

Writing Prompt: The Three Sisters were suggesting different names for the baby. What are your ideas? Write a letter to Jain to persuade her to select your boy and/or girl name for her new baby.

Lesson Plan 14: *Castle Waiting: The Lucky Road* by Linda Medley

Chapter 4—"The Caged Heart"

Unit/Curricular Connection: Folk and fairy tales, medieval times/literature

Grade Level: Grades 4–6 and high school for comparative literature

Objective: By the end of the lesson, students will learn how Jain's relationship with her daughter develops.

Direct Teaching:

1. Review the characters and plot from "Labors of Love."

2. Define vocabulary term: *efficacy*.

3. Reading of the story can be done independently, with partners, or as a whole class; you will have to decide based on grade level and reading ability. Stop periodically during the story to check for comprehension. After reading the story, have the students complete the reflection questions.

Reflection Questions:

1. Lady Jain names her baby after her father. What does this say about her relationship with her father?

2. In the middle of the story there is a flashback to when Jain is born. What do you think is the purpose of the flashback?

3. What is the importance of the gift Henry gives to Jain and her baby?

4. Why do you suppose Lady Jain takes Pindar for a walk around the castle?

Activities: Dinah is usually in the kitchen making meals for the entire group at Castle Waiting. Research medieval foods and prepare the recipes. Have a class medieval feast.

Lesson Plan 15: *Castle Waiting: The Lucky Road* by Linda Medley

Chapter 5—"Cavalier"

Unit/Curricular Connection: Folk and fairy tales, medieval times/literature

Grade Level: Grades 4–6 and high school for comparative literature

Objective: By the end of the lesson, students will know about the returning visitor to the castle and about Lady Jain's childhood.

Direct Teaching:

1. Review the characters and plot from "The Caged Heart."

2. Define vocabulary term: *cavalier.*

3. Reading of the story can be done independently, with partners, or as a whole class; you will have to decide based on grade level and reading ability. Stop periodically during the story to check for comprehension. After reading the story, have the students complete the reflection questions.

Reflection Questions:

1. What evidence does the book provide that Simon is learning to read?

2. Based on the story, how do we know that the visitor to the castle is not a stranger?

3. Chess visits Henry, and notices the rattle and baby toys that Henry is making. Based on this evidence, what do you think is on Henry's mind?

4. Jain is called Lisunka by Chess. What does this indicate about Jain's past? How does he know her?

5. The hourglasses represent a flashback in the story. From the flashback, what is learned about Lady Jain's childhood?

6. Why do you suppose Lady Jain gives Henry the baby to watch while she is drying the dishes?

Activities: In the flashback, Mr. Solander and Mr. Hencklemann talk about how the merchant class will be the ruling class. Research the class system that existed during medieval times. Who was at the top of the social and economic structure, and who was at the bottom?

Lesson Plan 16: *Castle Waiting: The Lucky Road* by Linda Medley

Chapter 6—"City Mouse, Country Mouse Part One"

Unit/Curricular Connection: Folk and fairy tales, medieval times/literature

Grade Level: Grades 4–6 and high school for comparative literature

Objective: By the end of the lesson, students will be introduced to shopping during medieval times and learn more about how the characters in the castle get their supplies.

Direct Teaching:

1. Review the characters and plot from "Cavalier."

2. Define vocabulary terms: *cowardly, stench, vermin,* and *geriatrics.*

3. Reading of the story can be done independently, with partners, or as a whole class; you will have to decide based on grade level and reading ability. Stop periodically during the story to check for comprehension. After reading the story, have the students complete the reflection questions.

Reflection Questions:

1. Based on the story, why do you think Chess always teases Rackham by calling him "Beaky"?

2. How does Wymbdon take care of those who break the law?

3. Based on the story, how do Chess and Rackham show their affection for the ladies of the castle?

4. Based on what you read, how does shopping during medieval times differ from modern times?

Activities: During medieval times, since so many people could not read, shopkeepers had pictures or symbols of what they sold hanging above their stores. For example, a picture of a fish would be hung up above a store that sold seafood. Research the types of stores that existed during medieval times and create signs that might have hung above their doors.

Lesson Plan 17: *Castle Waiting: The Lucky Road* by Linda Medley

Chapter 7—"City Mouse, Country Mouse Part Two"

Unit/Curricular Connection: Folk and fairy tales, medieval times/literature

Grade Level: Grades 4–6 and high school for comparative literature

Objective: By the end of the lesson, students will know more about city community life and the dangers of traveling in medieval times.

Direct Teaching:

1. Review the characters and plot from "City Mouse, Country Mouse."

2. Define vocabulary terms: *existent, militia, martial, mercy, eligible, mundane,* and *damsel.*

3. Reading of the story can be done independently, with partners, or as a whole class; you will have to decide based on grade level and reading ability. Stop periodically during the story to check for comprehension. After reading the story, have the students complete the reflection questions.

Reflection Questions:

1. What makes Sally a strong person in character?

2. Why do "One-Arm" Joe, Will Varlett, and Diesis want Rackham to join the poker game? What makes these characters seem so suspicious?

3. What were some dangers of traveling on the roads during medieval times?

4. Based on the story, why do you think Sally warns Rackham and Chess to "keep your hands on your purse-strings?"

5. At the end of the story, Rackham makes a toast "to more good changes." Predict some changes that might occur at Castle Waiting in the next story.

Activities: At the end of book two, everyone in the castle is having a tea party for fun. They did not have electricity, televisions, stereos, or video games. Research what types of games and entertainment were available during medieval times and then have a medieval game day.

Electronic Resource for Teachers:

Middle Ages: www.learner.org/exhibits/middleages/

Appendix: 100 Graphic Novels

To help you continue in your quest to stock your shelves with worthy graphic novels, we offer this list of 100 graphic novels, sorted by age level and including interest areas, review sources, publishing information, and author names. As we have repeated throughout this book, there are thousands of graphic novels in print, with more being published each month. No book can comprehensively detail them all. We offer, instead, a hundred that we think are suitable for school libraries and various levels.

All Ages

Title	Interest Area	Author	Publisher (Publication Date)	Reviews
Comic Adventures of Boots	Humorous fiction, cats	Kitamura	St. Martins Press (2002)	*Publishers Weekly*
Marvel Masterworks: Daredevil	Daredevil, superheroes	Lee	Marvel Books (2001)	*School Library Journal*
Phoenix: A Tale of the Future	Fantasy, science fiction, adventure	Tezuka	Viz Communications (2002)	*Publishers Weekly*
Spirited Away	fantasy, action and adventure, magic	Miyazaki	Viz Communications (2002)	*Publishers Weekly*

Elementary School

Title	Interest Area	Author	Publisher (Publication Date)	Reviews
Astro Boy Volume 1	Children's stories, manga, robots	Tezuka	Dark Horse Comics (2001)	Artbomb.net, Diamond Bookshelf
Cave-In	Children's stories, adventure	Ralph	Highwater Books (1999)	Artbomb.net
Climbing Out	Children's stories, animal stories	Ralph	Brian Ralph (2003)	Artbomb.net
Courtney Crumin and the Night Things	Children's books, fantasy	Naifeh	Oni Press (2003)	Diamond Bookshelf
The Essential Uncanny X-Men[2]	X-Men, superheroes	Lee	Marvel Comics (2003)	*School Library Journal*
Good Bye, Chunky Rice	Children's stories, adventure, friendship	Thompson	Top Shelf Productions (2001)	Artbomb.net, *Publishers Weekly*
Leave It to Chance: Shaman's Rain[2]	Fantasy, mystery, fiction	Robinson	Image (2003)	*Publishers Weekly*
Louis: Red Letter Day	Children's stories, adventure	Metaphrog	Metaphrog (2000)	Artbomb.net
Manga Mania: How to Draw Japanese Comics[3]	Drawing-reference, manga	Hart	Watson-Guptill (2002)	YALSA Quick Pick
Speed Racer: Born to Race	Auto racing fiction, action and adventure	Yune	DC Comics/Wildstorm (2000)	Diamond Bookshelf
Thieves and Kings[1]	Magic, action and adventure, wizards and wizardry	Oakley	I Box (2001)	Diamond Bookshelf
Ultimate X-Men[1]	X-Men, superheroes	Sanderson	DK (2000)	*School Library Journal*

1—This title is appropriate for elementary and middle schools.
2—This title is appropriate for its designated age level and any higher age levels.
3—This title is recommended for upper elementary students.

Middle School

Title	Interest Area	Author	Publisher (Publication Date)	Reviews
9-11 Artists Respond[2]	9-11 tragedy	Various	Dark Horse Comics (2002)	*School Library Journal*, Diamond Bookshelf
9-11: The World's Finest Comic Book Writers and Artists Tell Stories to Remember[2]	9-11 tragedy	Various	DC Comics (2002)	*School Library Journal*, Diamond Bookshelf
Amazing Spider-Man: Coming Home[2]	Superheroes, Superman	Straczynski	Marvel Comics (2002)	YALSA Quick Pick
Amy Unbounded: Belondweg Blossoming[2]	Fantasy, coming-of-age, fiction	Hartman	Pug House Press (2003)	Artbomb.net
Anime Mania: How to Draw Characters for Japanese Animation[2]	Drawing –reference, anime	Hart	Watson-Guptill (2002)	YALSA Quick Pick
Aqua Knight Volume 2[2]	Manga, action and adventure, fantasy	Kishiro	Viz Communications (2002)	Diamond Bookshelf
Barnum![2]	Circus, comics, American history	Chaykin	DC Comics (2003)	*Publishers Weekly*
Batman: Hong Kong[2]	Batman, superheroes, martial arts	Moench	DC Comics (2003)	*Publishers Weekly*
The Big O Volume 1[2]	Action and adventure, science fiction	Ariga	Viz Communications (2003)	Diamond Bookshelf
The Cartoon History of the Universe[2]	History, ancient history, general history	Gonick	Doubleday (2002)	*Publishers Weekly*
The Cartoon History of the Universe II[2]	History, ancient history, general history	Gonick	Main Street Books (1994)	*Publishers Weekly*

Middle School (*cont.*)

Title	Interest Area	Author	Publisher (Publication Date)	Reviews
Creature Tech[2]	Science fiction, creationism	Tennapel	Top Shelf (2002)	YALSA pick, *Publishers Weekly, Booklist*
Crystal Ball[2]	Mystery, espionage, fiction	Rucka	Oni Press (2003)	*Publishers Weekly*
Daredevil Yellow[2]	Daredevil, superheroes	Miller	Marvel Books (2002)	*School Library Journal*
Daredevil: Visionaries[2]	Daredevil, superheroes	Miller	Marvel Books (2000)	*School Library Journal*
Daredevil: Visionaries Volume 2[2]	Daredevil, superheroes	Miller	Marvel Books (2001)	*School Library Journal*
Daredevil: Visionaries Volume 3[2]	Daredevil, superheroes	Miller	Marvel Books (2001)	*School Library Journal*
Days Like This[2]	Music, fiction, girls' stories	Torres	Oni Press (2003)	*Publishers Weekly*, 2004 YALSA Nominee
Delicate Creatures[2]	Fantasy, folk and fairy tales	Straczynski	Image Comics (2001)	Diamond Bookshelf
Dignifying Science[2]	Science, biography	Ottaviani, Severinson, et al.	G.T. Labs (2000)	*Publishers Weekly*
Fagin the Jew[2]	Racism, Jewish life, fiction	Eisner	Doubleday (2003)	*School Library Journal*
Fallout[2]	Nuclear science, biography, humorous fiction	Ottaviani, Lieber, et al.	G.T. Labs (2001)	Diamond Bookshelf
The Fatal Bullet: The Assassination of President Garfield[2]	American history, true crime	Geary	NBM Publishing, Inc. (2003)	*Publishers Weekly*

Middle School (*cont.*)

Title	Interest Area	Author	Publisher (Publication Date)	Reviews
The Frank Book[2]	Fantasy, humorous fiction	Woodring	Fantagraphics (2003)	*Publishers Weekly*
Girl Genius-Book One: Agatha Hereodyne and the Beetleburg Clank[2]	Humorous fiction, romance stories, fantasy	Foglio	Airship Entertainment (2003)	Diamond Bookshelf
Hammer of the Gods: Mortal Enemy[2]	Action and adventure, fiction	Oeming	Image Comics (2003)	Diamond Bookshelf
Heaven Sword & Dragon Sabre[2]	Action and adventure, martial arts fiction	Ma	ComicsOne (2002)	Diamond Bookshelf
Hero Bear and the Kid: Volume 1, Inheritance[2]	Literature, fantasy	Kunkel	Astonish Comics (2003)	YALSA pick
Hopeless Savages: Ground Zero[2]	Humorous fiction, teenagers, families	Van Meter	Oni Press (2003)	*Publishers Weekly*
Iron Wok Jan! Volume 1[2]	Cooking, humorous fiction, manga	Saijyo	ComicsOne (2003)	Artbomb.net
Jack the Ripper[2]	History, biography, true crime	Geary	NBM Publishing, Inc. (2003)	*Publishers Weekly*
Jingle Belle's Cool Yule[2]	Humorous fiction, fantasy, action and adventure	Dini	Oni Press (2002)	Diamond Bookshelf
JLA: Tower of Babel[2]	Superheroes, action and adventure	Waid	DC Comics (2002)	YALSA Quick Pick
Joan Book 1[2]	Hundred Years' War fiction, action and adventure	Yasuhiko	Comicsone.com (2001)	Diamond Bookshelf

Middle School (*cont.*)

Title	Interest Area	Author	Publisher (Publication Date)	Reviews
Kin: The Descent of Man[2]	Action and adventure	Frank	Image Comics (2001)	Diamond Bookshelf
King Volume 1[2]	Martin Luther King Jr., biography	Anderson	Fantagraphics (1994)	Artbomb.net, *Publishers Weekly*
The Legendary Couple[2]	Action and adventure, fiction	Cha	ComicsOne (2003)	Diamond Bookshelf
Mad About Super Heroes[2]	Superheroes	Meglin	DC Comics (2002)	YALSA Quick Pick
Metropolis[2]	Science fiction and fantasy	Tezuka	Dark Horse Comics (2003)	YALSA pick, *Publishers Weekly*
New X-Men: New Worlds[2]	X-Men, superheroes	Morrison	Marvel Books (2002)	*School Library Journal*
Origin: The True Story of Wolverine[2]	Superheroes, wolverine	Jenkins	Marvel Comics (2002)	YALSA Quick Pick
The Path: Crisis of Faith[2]	Action and adventure, fiction	Marz	CrossGen Comics (2003)	Diamond Bookshelf
Pedro and Me[2]	AIDS, biography	Winick	Henry Holt (2000)	Artbomb.net, YALSA
Persepolis[2]	Adolescent stories, growing up, biography	Satrapi	Pantheon (2003)	Artbomb.net, *Publishers Weekly*
Red Rocket 7[2]	Science fiction and fantasy	Allred	Dark Horse (1998)	YALSA pick
Samurai Noir[2]	Martial arts, fiction	Oeming	Image Comics (2003)	*Publishers Weekly*
Shadow Star Volume 1[2]	Manga, science fiction, action and adventure	Kitoh	Dark Horse Comics (2001)	Diamond Bookshelf

Middle School (*cont.*)

Title	Interest Area	Author	Publisher (Publication Date)	Reviews
Storm Riders Volume 1[2]	Fantasy, swords and sorcery, martial arts –fiction	Ma	ComicsOne (2002)	Diamond Bookshelf
Strum & Drang: Great Moments in Rock & Roll[2]	Music, fiction, entertainment	Orff	Alternative Comics (2003)	YALSA pick, *School Library Journal*
Ultimate X-Men: World Tour[2]	X-Men, superheroes	Millar	Marvel Books (2002)	*School Library Journal*
Usagi Yojimbo: Grasscutter & Journey to Atsuta Shrine[2]	Science fiction, action and adventure	Sakai	Dark Horse (2002)	YALSA pick
The X-Men: Mutant Genesis[2]	X-Men, superheroes	Claremont	Marvel Comics (2002)	*School Library Journal*
X-Men Legends Volume II: The Dark Phoenix Saga[2]	X-Men, superheroes	Claremont	Marvel Books (2003)	*School Library Journal*
Zero Girl[2]	Humor, love stories fiction	Kieth	DC Comics (2001)	Diamond Bookshelf

1—This title is appropriate for elementary and middle schools.
2—This title is appropriate for its designated age level and any higher age levels.
3—This title is recommended for upper elementary students.

High School

Title	Interest Area	Author	Publisher (Publication Date)	Reviews
9-11 Emergency Relief	Social studies, current events	Mason, Eisner, et al.	Alternative Comics (2002)	*School Library Journal*
The Adventures of Barry Ween, Boy Genius	Humorous fiction	Winick	Oni Press (1999)	Artbomb. net, YALSA
The Barefoot Serpent	Family, grief, suicide	Kurosawa (Japanese film director) and Morse	Top Shelf Productions (2003)	*VOYA*
Blankets	Relationships, biography	Thompson	Top Shelf (2003)	Artbomb.net, *Publishers Weekly*
The Cartoon Guide to Sex	Science, health	Gonick and DeVault	Harperperennial Library (1999)	*Publishers Weekly*
Catch As Catch Can	Humorous fiction	Cook	Highwater Books (1999)	Artbomb.net
The Collected Hutch Owen	Humorous fiction	Hart	Top Shelf (2000)	Artbomb.net
Daredevil: Underboss	Daredevil, superheroes	Bendis	Marvel Books (2002)	School Library Journal
Fax from Sarajevo	Modern war, Yugoslavia, biography	Kubert	Dark Horse Comics (1998)	Artbomb.net, *Publishers Weekly*
From Hell	World history, Victorian England, true crime	Moore and Campbell	Eddie Campbell Comics (2000)	Diamond Bookshelf
Grasshopper and the Ant	Humorous fiction	Kurtzman	Denis Kitchen Publishing (2001)	Artbomb.net
The Great Comic Book Heroes	Comic books, social critiques	Feiffer	Fantagraphics Books (2003)	*School Library Journal, Publishers Weekly*

High School (*cont.*)

Title	Interest Area	Author	Publisher (Publication Date)	Reviews
Great Moments in Rock & Roll	Postwar Sarajevo, nonfiction	Sacco	Drawn and Quarterly (2003)	Publishers Weekly
Hawaiian Dick Volume 1: Byrd of Paradise	Crime stories, mystery	Moore	Image Comics (2003)	*Publishers Weekly*
I Never Liked You	Relationships, biography	Brown	Drawn and Quarterly (2001)	Artbomb.net
Maus: A Survivor's Tale	History, biography	Spiegelman	Pantheon Books (1997)	Pulitizer Prize, *Publishers Weekly*
No More Shaves	Human story collections, elderly	Greenburger	Fantagraphics (2001)	Artbomb.net, *Publishers Weekly*
Notes from a Defeatist	War, story collections	Sacco	Fantagraphics (2003)	*Publishers Weekly*
Onegai Teacher	Fantasy, manga, science fiction	Seto	ComicsOne (2003)	*Publishers Weekly*
Palestine	Political science, social studies	Sacco	Fantagraphics Books (2002)	*Publishers Weekly*
Quimby the Mouse	Fiction	Ware	Fantagraphics Books (2003)	*Publishers Weekly*
Rebound, Volume 1	Basketball, humor, drama	Nishiyama	Tokyopop (2003)	*VOYA*
Road to Perdition	Mystery	Collins	Pocket Books (2002)	*Publishers Weekly*
Route 666: Highway to Horror	Murder, drama	Bedard	CrossGen Comics (2003)	*VOYA*
Safe Area Gorazde	War, biography, Bosnia, ethnic cleansing	Sacco	Fantagraphics (2000)	*Publishers Weekly*
Sandman Volume 1: Preludes & Nocturnes	Fantasy, action and adventure	Gaiman	DC Comics/Vertigo (1991)	*Library Journal, Publishers Weekly*

High School (*cont.*)

Title	Interest Area	Author	Publisher (Publication Date)	Reviews
Speechless	War and warfare, fiction	Mills	Top Shelf Productions (2002)	*Publishers Weekly*
Vogelein: Clockwork Faerie	Fantasy, adventure	Irwin	Fiery Studios (2003)	*VOYA*
War Junkie	War, war story collections	Sacco	Fantagraphics (1995)	*Publishers Weekly*
Yossel, April 19, 1943	World War II, Warsaw Ghetto uprising	Kubert	ibooks (2003)	Artbomb.net

Glossary

Following is a glossary of terms used throughout this book that have particular meaning when applied to the graphic novel/comic book world. Words in boldface within definitions are themselves defined in the glossary.

alternative: A term used as an adjective, usually to describe anything that is *not* **mainstream**. Its use connotes a qualitative difference in storytelling styles, subject matter, and form. It comes from the dominance of the large, corporate publishers, causing smaller publishers to label themselves as the "alternative" reading choice.

anime: A Japanese term that refers to animation, such as cartoons on television or in the movies. Outside Japan, the term refers not to animation in general but rather specifically to animated programming in the Japanese style. (See **manga** for more information.)

artist: Comic books usually have three kinds of art (beyond the art of writing) associated with them. Historically, the three functions were performed by three individuals separate from the writer and were distinct job titles. It is now common to see the tasks performed by one or more people in any combination, sometimes in combination with the writing as well. A **penciler** does the initial work of laying out the page based on the script. He or she creates each panel, places the figures and settings in the panels, etc. The penciled pages are then passed to an **inker**, who uses black ink to render the pencils into fuller, rounder tones. The inker usually adds depth and shadow to the images—a good inker will bring out and enhance the strengths of a penciler's artwork. A **colorist** takes the inked pages and adds color. There are, of course, exceptions to this general workflow: Comics are produced in black and white, with gray tones instead of colors, etc. Some comics are painted in full color, rendering further artists moot. A comic book can have multiple pencilers, inkers, and colorists, or one person can perform any and all of these functions.

captions: Boxes on a comic book page that contain text. Like **word balloons**, they are usually subjected to a variety of effects to create different "moods" or concepts. A caption can be any shape, size, or color. While sometimes used to convey dialogue, they are more often used to impart a character's thoughts or as a narrative device.

cartoonist: A title used by many **artists** who perform multiple tasks in the creation of a **comic**, including the writing. The term connotes an holistic approach to the creation of a comic, with the implication that the work is predominantly the creation of a single vision.

"cartoony": An admittedly vague and subjective term used to describe a style of art that is typically characterized by clean lines and representational, iconic images rather than exacting replicas of reality.

collected edition: Another term for **trade paperback**.

colorist: See **artist**.

comic: Used interchangeably with **comic book**.

comic book: Traditionally, a comic book was a stapled, magazinelike product that told a serialized story or anthologized many stories over a period of months and years. The term has evolved to describe *any* **format** that uses the combination of words and pictures to convey a story, and thus is accurate when applied to both the medium itself *and* the **periodical** form. As a result, all **graphic novels** are comic books, but not all comic books are graphic novels. See also **pamphlet**.

comic book specialty store: A retail store that primarily sells **comic books** and related merchandise. Similar to a bookstore or hobby store in that the establishment is focused on a particular type of product, serves a specific clientele, and is usually staffed by employees who possess a great deal of personal knowledge about the products they carry.

comics: The plural of comic is typically used as a singular (as "politics" is) to refer to the entire medium or industry. Hence, "comics industry" or "comics **creators**." This is usually employed to avoid the unintentional consequences of using the adjective "comic," which implies comedic content. (For example, "the comic industry" might be misinterpreted as meaning "an industry that is funny," while "the comics industry" can mean only "the industry that creates **comic books**.")

comix: A word coined in the 1960s to describe titles that nowadays would be considered **alternative**. The comix were titles created as a reaction to the juvenilization of comics compelled by Congress in the 1950s, and usually contained adult humor and sexual and political topics.

creative team: This term describes the individual(s) who created the **comic book** in question. A **writer**, **artist**, **letterer**, and **editor** will usually be credited in the comic book. Note that these functions can be performed by one or more people, acting collectively or individually. A comic book may have one writer and multiple artists, for example, or may be the creation of a single person.

creators: See **creative team**.

editor: An individual charged with the editorial functions for a **comic book**. Depending on the publisher and the **creative team**, the editor may have broad control over the content and direction of the story, may act as a manager who shepherds the story through the creative process, or may function as an "extra set of eyes" to catch errors and glitches in the process.

Eisner Awards: Familiarly known as "the Eisners," the annual Will Eisner Comic Industry Awards recognize the finest stories, publications, and creators in the medium. The awards are named for Will Eisner, the **writer/artist** credited with creating the graphic storytelling format of the **graphic novel**, which showed the world that **comics** were more than just "funny books" that told only superhero stories.

format: A generic term that encompasses all the various ways in which a **comic book** story can be told and sold. **Periodicals**, **graphic novels**, and **trade paperbacks** are all comic book formats.

GN: An abbreviation for **graphic novel**.

graphic novel: Used to describe the specific format of a **comic book** that has greater production values and longer narrative. Can also describe the **trade paperback** format. The graphic novel is more like a traditional novel, in that it is published on an independent schedule. It is longer in format than a **periodical** and typically contains a complete story unto itself. Graphic novels usually have higher production values than the typical stapled comic book; they may be squarebound, for example, with cardstock covers. Some may be hardcover volumes. Although a graphic novel usually stands on its own as a complete story, it is possible to have an **ongoing series** or **limited series** of graphic novels telling a single story or series of related stories. A typical abbreviation in the industry for graphic novel is "**GN**," usually used as part of a title to indicate to a reader or browser that the title in question is not a periodical.

gutter: The empty space between **panels** on a **comic book page**.

Harvey Awards: The Harveys are unique among the awards given in the **comics** medium in that they are voted on entirely by professionals in the industry, meaning that winners are honored for excellence by their peers. This prestigious award is named after Harvey Kurtzman, cofounder of *MAD* magazine and a seminal influence in the development of comics as a versatile storytelling vehicle.

HC: An abbreviation for hardcover.

independent (or "indy") : Initially used to describe any comic book that was not published by the two major publishers, DC and Marvel. The term has come to encompass a broad range of material.

inker: See **artist**.

layout: The design elements that make up a **comic book page**. For example, an **artist** may choose to use **panels** without borders, or round panels, or many tiny panels to evoke a particular mood or feeling.

letterer: The individual who places word balloons and captions on the finished artwork and fills them with words based on the script. Letterers also often provide the sound effects prevalent in comics, though sometimes the **artist** will render them.

limited series: A **maxi-series** or **mini-series**.

mainstream: In the comic book industry, this refers to **comic books** that appeal not to the mass market mainstream but rather to the mainstream *comic book* reader. As a result, the term usually denotes superhero comics and similar fare.

manga: The Japanese word for "**comic book**." Outside Japan, the term has come to refer specifically to comic books produced in the style most associated with Japanese comic books. Some elements of this style include exaggerated facial expressions and proportions to convey emotion, focus on the eyes, the use of trailing lines ("speed lines") to evoke swift movement, and deliberate pacing that can make actions occur over many **panels** or **pages**.

manwha: A word that is typically used to describe **comic books** from China or Korea.

maxi-series: A **comic book** series that is scheduled to run only a certain number of issues (usually more than six) and then end. An analogy would be a television program such as *Taken*, which ended after a specific number of airings and after telling a specific story. A maxi-series can have a frequency from weekly to semiannual, but most are at least bimonthly. It is possible to have a maxi-series made up of **graphic novels**.

mini-series: A **comic book** series that is scheduled to run only a certain number of issues (usually six or fewer) and then end. An analogy would be a television program such as *Roots*, which ended after a specific number of airings and after telling a specific story. A mini-series can have a frequency from weekly to semiannual, but most are at least bimonthly. It is possible to have a mini-series made up of **graphic novels**.

nine-panel grid: A particular **layout** choice that is immediately recognizable, in which a **page** is divided evenly into three tiers of three equal-sized **panels**.

OGN: An abbreviation for original **graphic novel**, often used to differentiate a graphic novel that contains a wholly new story from a **trade paperback**.

ongoing series: A **comic book** series that has no ending planned and will continue until sales dictate its cancellation. An example is *Action Comics*, from DC Comics, a series that has been published nearly continuously since 1938. An analogy would be a television program such as *ER*, which runs until it is no longer profitable or other factors dictate its conclusion. Ongoing series can have a frequency from weekly to semiannual. Most are monthly or bimonthly.

page: A page is made up of **panels**. Each page in a **comic book**, when rendered properly, is a piece of art greater than the sum of its parts. A good comic book **artist** will consider pacing, time, and story flow when composing the page, so that the page conveys the mood and tone of the story appropriately. A page made up of only one panel is called a "**splash page**." Historically, a splash page was the first page in a comic book and listed that issue's title and creator credits. In modern comics, any page can be a splash page, and the credits and title can similarly appear anywhere in the issue. In some cases, a single panel will be made of *two* pages, stretching across the fold of the comic. This is called a "**two-page spread**."

pamphlet: A term used by some to describe the original **comic book** form, that of a slim, magazinelike periodical, not designed for long-term use or wear and tear. The term is considered derisive by some. Compare **periodical**.

panel: A panel is a portion of a **comic book page** that is separated from other portions of the page. A single panel typically represents a moment in time, a single action, or a setting. The panel is the basic unit of storytelling in a comic book. Panels can contain **word balloons**, **captions**, artwork, or any combination of the above. Panels are usually square or rectangular, with a border of some sort to separate them from other panels. However, they may be any shape, any size, and may or may not contain borders at all. The construction of panels is one of the most basic creative decisions an **artist** makes.

penciler: See **artist**.

periodical: A term used by some to describe the original **comic book** form, which was slim and magazinelike, not designed for long-term use or wear and tear. Compare **pamphlet**.

"photo-realistic": An admittedly vague and subjective term used to describe an art style in which the artist makes use of models and photo references to attempt to mimic reality as closely as possible. An excellent example is Alex Ross's artwork (*Marvels*, *Kingdom Come*).

"realistic": An admittedly vague and subjective term used to describe what is probably the most familiar type of art for a newcomer to comics. In this style, the artist forgoes representational images and strives to create a world that resembles our own, albeit greatly simplified.

Reuben Award: Voted on and presented by the National Cartoonists Society, the Reuben Award is bestowed upon illustrators in numerous categories, including comic strips, **comic books**, and animation. Winners have included many of the world's most famous cartoonists. The Reubens are named for legendary cartoonist Rube Goldberg, who founded the Society.

SC: An abbreviation for softcover.

shojo: A **manga** that is written for and aimed at a young, female audience.

splash page: See **page**.

story arc: A specific story told in an **ongoing series** over a course of many issues. Sometimes called a "**mini-series** within a series." The story arc will often have its own title, with each issue being a "chapter."

TP(B): An abbreviation for **trade paperback**.

trade: Shorthand for **trade paperback**.

trade paperback: In the comic book industry, the term is used differently than in the book trade. A **comic book** trade paperback is a squarebound edition that collects and reprints a **mini-series**, **maxi-series**, or **story arc** in this sturdier format, giving readers a complete story at one time rather than over a period of months. Sometimes a trade paperback may collect stories that are not interconnected but rather are related by some theme. Many trade paperbacks also contain additional material, such as an introduction or foreword, or character sketches. Usually abbreviated "**TP**."

two-page spread: See **page**.

word balloon: Word balloons are the text-filled bubbles that contain dialogue. There are many shapes and forms for word balloons. The average word balloon is a black-bordered oval, with black text on a white background. Word balloons that seem "fluffy" or cloudlike usually convey a character's thoughts (much like italics in genre fiction). Jagged word balloons can indicate surprise or outrage. In recent years, colors, shading, and other techniques have been applied both to word balloons and the letters within them to get across a diversity of ideas: telepathy, radio broadcasts, the thunderous speech of godlike characters, whispers, etc. Note that most **comic books** are lettered entirely in uppercase, with emphasis denoted by the use of boldface.

writer: The writer, naturally, writes the **comic book**. This is not, however limited to "writing the words in the balloons," as many newcomers often think, but rather requires developing and putting down on paper the entire story in such a way that the **artist** can then interpret it into visuals for the reader. It is possible to have multiple writers on a single comic book. Sometimes one writer will plot the comic, and a second will write the dialogue after the fact. In other cases, many writers may plot a comic book together, with one of them (or another writer) supplying the dialogue.

References

Block, C. (1999). Comprehension: Crafting understanding. In L. Gambrell, L. Morrow, S. Neuman, and M. Pressley (Eds.), *Best practices in literacy instruction* (pp. 98–118). New York: Guilford.

Burmark, L. (2002). *Visual Literacy: Learn to see, see to learn.* Alexandria, VA: Association for Supervision and Curriculum Development.

Crawford, P. (2003). Thought bubbles: Beyond *Maus*: Using graphic novels to support social studies standards. *Knowledge Quest 31*(31).

Dvorak, T. (2002, July 31). Graphic novels give weight to comic books. *The Record*, F6.

Gardner, H. (1991). *The unschooled mind: How children think and how schools should teach.* New York: Basic Books.

Gitlin, T. (2001). *Media unlimited: How the torrent of images and sounds overwhelms our lives.* New York: Metropolitan.

Goldsmith, F. (n.d.). Teen Read Week, http://archive.ala.org:80/teenread/trw/index.html (accessed October 25, 2003).

Hibbing, A., & Rankin-Erickson, J. (2003, May). A picture is worth a thousand words: using visual images to improve comprehension for middle school struggling readers. *The Reading Teacher*, 758.

Hobbs, R. (2001, May). Improving reading comprehension by using media literacy activities. *Voices from the Middle*, 44–51.

Hunter, S. (2002, July 21). Every picture impels the story; graphic novels, providing fluid segues into film. *The Washington Post*, p. G1.

Lavin, M. R. (1998). Comic books and graphic novels for libraries: What to buy. *Serials Review*, *24*(2).

McCloud, S. (1994). *Understanding comics.* New York: Perennial.

Schwartz, G. (2002). Graphic novels for multiple literacies. *Journal of Adolescent & Adult Literacy 46*(3).

Smith, M. (2002). *"Reading don't fix no chevy's": Literacy in the lives of young men.* Portsmouth, NH: Heinemann.

Bibliography

Introduction

Chabon, M. *The Amazing Adventures of Kavalier and Clay*. New York: Picador, 2001.

David, P. *Aquaman*. New York: DC Comics, 1993.

Fox, G. *The Golden Age Flash Archives*. New York: DC Comics, 1999.

Gownley, J. *Amelia Rules*. Harrisburg, PA: Renaissance Press, 2001.

Medley, L. *Castle Waiting*. Columbus, OH: Olio Press, 2000.

Smith, J. *Bone*. Columbus, OH: Cartoon Books, 1995.

Takeuchi, N. *Sailor Moon*. Los Angeles: TokyoPop, 2000.

Thompson, J. *Scary Godmother*. San Antonio, TX: Sirius Entertainment, 1997.

Chapter 1

Collins, M. *Road to Perdition*. New York: Pocket Books, 2002.

Cruse, H. *Stuck Rubber Baby*. New York: DC Comics, 2000.

Geary, R. *The Mystery of Mary Rogers*. New York: NBM Publishing, 2003.

Giardino, V. *A Jew in Communist Prague*. New York: NBM Publishing, 2003.

Gonick, L. *The Cartoon History of the Universe II*. Mansfield, OH: Main Street Books, 1994.

Kubert, J. *Fax from Sarajevo*. Milwaukie, OR: Dark Horse Comics, 1998.

Russell, C. *Fairy Tales of Oscar Wilde: The Selfish Giants & the Star Child*. New York: NBM Publishing, 2003.

Sacco, J. *Palestine*. Seattle: Fantagraphics Books, 2002.

Sacco, J. *Safe Area Gorazde*. Seattle: Fantagraphics Books, 2002.

Speigelman, A. *Maus*. New York: Pantheon Books, 1986.

Chapter 2

Action Comics. New York: DC Comics, 1938– .

Bagge, P. *Hate*. Seattle: Fantagraphics Books, 1993.

McCloud, S. *Understanding Comics*. New York: Perennial, 1994.

Ross, A. *Kingdom Come*. New York: DC Comics, 1997.

Ross, A. *Marvels*. New York: Marvel Books, 2001.

Sacco, J. *Palestine*. Seattle: Fantagraphics Books, 2002.

Smith, J. *Bone*. Columbus, OH: Cartoon Books, 1996.

Speigelman, A. *Maus*. New York: Pantheon Books, 1986.

Superman. New York: DC Comics, 1939– .

Chapter 3

Atangan, P. *The Yellow Jar.* New York: NBM Publishing, 2002.

Chadwick, P. *Concrete: Killer Smile.* Milwaukie, OR: Dark Horse Comics, 1995.

Drechsler, D. *Summer of Love.* Montreal: Drawn & Quarterly, 2003.

Eisner, W. *Moby Dick.* New York: NBM Publishing, 1998.

Eisner, W. *Sundiata: A Legend of Africa.* New York: NBM Publishing, 2002.

Fujishima, K. *Oh My Goddess! Wrong Number.* Milwaukie, OR: Dark Horse Comics, 2002.

Gaiman, N. *Sandman.* New York: DC Comics, 1993.

Gaiman, N. *The Wolves in the Walls.* New York: HarperCollins, 2003.

Gownley, J. *Amelia Rules.* Harrisburg, PA: Renaissance Press, 2001.

Kesel, B. *Meridian.* Oldsmar, FL: CrossGeneration Comics, 2001.

Kobayashi, M. *What's Michael? Michael's Favorite Spot.* Milwaukie, OR: Dark Horse Comics, 2002.

Kochalka, J. *Monkey vs. Robot.* Marietta, GA: Top Shelf Productions, 2000.

Kochalka, J. *Pinky & Stinky.* Marietta, GA: Top Shelf Productions, 2002.

Koslowski, R. *three fingers.* Marietta, GA: Top Shelf Productions, 2002.

Lee, S. *X-Men.* New York: Marvel Books, 1963– .

Medley, L. *Castle Waiting.* Columbus, OH: Olio Press, 2000.

Miller, F. *300.* Milwaukie, OR: Dark Horse Maverick, 1999.

Millionaire, T. *Sock Monkey: Glass Doorknob.* Milwaukie, OR: Dark Horse Maverick, 2002.

Robin, T., and L. Trondheim. *Li'l Santa.* New York: NBM Publishing, 2002.

Sakai, S. *Usagi Yojimbo.* Milwaukie, OR: Dark Horse Comics, 1999.

Shanower, E. *Age of Bronze: A Thousand Ships.* Orange, CA: Image Comics, 2001.

Smith, J. *Bone.* Columbus, OH: Cartoon Books, 1995.

Speigelman, A. *Maus.* New York: Pantheon Books, 1986.

Superman. New York: DC Comics, 1939– .

Takahashi, R. *Ranma ½.* San Francisco: Viz Communications, 2002.

Thompson, J. *Scary Godmother.* San Antonio, TX: Sirius Entertainment, 1999.

Thompson, J. *Scary Godmother: The Boo Flu.* San Antonio, TX: Sirius Entertainment, 2000.

Thompson, J. *Scary Godmother: The Mystery Date.* San Antonio, TX: Sirius Entertainment, 19999.

Torres, J., and J. Bone. *The Collected Alison Dare: Little Miss Adventures.* Portland, OR: Oni Press, 2002.

Usui, Y. *Crayon ShinChan.* Fremont, CA: ComicsOne, 2002.

Varon, S. *Sweaterweather.* Gainesville, FL: Alternative Comics, 2003.

Chapter 4

Nakazawa, K. *Barefoot Gen.* Philadelphia: New Society Publishers, 1986.

Pilkey, D. *Captain Underpants.* New York: Little Apple, 1997.

Tsuda, M. *Kare Kano.* San Francisco: Tokyopop, 2003.

Winick, J. *Pedro and Me: Friendship, Loss, and What I Learned.* New York: Henry Holt, 2000.

Chapter 5

Akamatsu, K. *Love Hina*. San Francisco: Tokyopop, 2002.

Aragones, S. *Groo*. Milwaukie, OR: Dark Horse Comics, 2000.

Aragones, S. *Groo and Rufferto*. Milwaukie, OR: Dark Horse Comics, 2000.

Batman Adventures. New York: DC Comics, 1993.

Bendis, B. *Ultimate Spider-Man*. New York: Marvel Books, 2002.

Busiek, K. *Astro City*. Orange, CA: Image Comics, 1997.

Busiek, K. *Marvels*. New York: Marvel Books, 2001.

Byrne, J. *Superman & Batman: Generations*. New York: DC Comics, 2000.

Clamp. *Chobits*. Los Angeles: TokyoPop, 2002.

Clowes, D. *Ghost World*. Seattle: Fantagraphics Books, 2001.

Crilley, M. *Akiko*. San Antonio, TX: Sirius Entertainment, 2001.

Eisner, W. *Comics & Sequential Art*. Tamarac, FL: Poorhouse Press, 1994.

Eisner, W. *A Contract with God: And Other Testament Stories*. New York: DC Comics, 2000.

Eisner, W. *Graphic Storytelling & Visual Narrative*. Tamarac, FL: Poorhouse Press, 1996.

Eisner, W. *Last Knight*. New York: NBM Publishing, 2003.

Eisner, W. *Moby Dick*. New York: NBM Publishing, 1998.

Eisner, W. *Princess and the Frog*. New York: NBM Publishing, 2003.

Eisner, W. *Sundiata: A Legend of Africa*. New York: NBM Publishing, 2002.

Essentials Series. New York: Marvel Comics, 1998.

Fujishima, K. *Oh My Goddess! Wrong Number*. Milwaukie, OR: Dark Horse Comics, 2002.

Fulop, S. *Archie Americana Series: Best of the 80s*. Mamaroneck, NY: Archie Comic Publications, 2001.

Gaiman, N. *Books of Magic*. New York: DC Comics, 1992.

Gaiman, N. *The Sandman*. New York: DC Comics, 1993.

Gonick, L. *The Cartoon History of the Universe II*. Mansfield, OH: Main Street Books, 1994.

Goscinny, R. *Asterix series*. Washington, DC: Mars Import, 1995.

Grahame, K. *Wind in the Willows*. New York: Aladdin Library, 1989.

Grayson, Devin K. *Batman: No Man's Land*. New York: DC Comics, 1999.

Groening, M. *Bart Simpson Collections*. New York: Perennial, 2002.

Groening, M. *Simpsons: Big Book of Bart Simpson*. New York: Perennial, 2002.

Hayashi, H. *How to Draw Manga*. Tokyo, Japan: Graphic Sha Publishing Company, 2003.

Herge. *Tintin*. New York: Little, Brown, 1979.

Hosler, J. *Clan Apis*. Columbus, OH: Active Synapse, 2000.

Hosler, J. *The Sandwalk Adventures*. Columbus, OH: Active Synapse, 2003.

James, R. *Leave It to Chance*. Orange, CA: Image Comics, 2002.

Jenkins, P. *Origin*. New York: Marvel Comics, 2002.

Kesel, B. *Meridian*. Oldsmar, FL: CrossGeneration Comics, 2001.

Kunkel, M. *Hero Bear and the Kid*. Los Angeles: Astonish Comics, 2001.

Lee, A. *Hobbit: An Illustrated Edition.* Boston: Houghton Mifflin, 1997.

Lee, S. *Amazing Spider-Man.* New York: Marvel Books, 2002.

Loeb, J. *Batman: The Long Halloween.* New York: DC Comics, 1999.

Loeb, J. *Superman For All Seasons.* New York: DC Comics, 1999.

Mack, D. *Kabuki.* Orange, CA: Image Comics, 2001.

Medley, L. *Castle Waiting: Curse of the Brambly Hedge.* Columbus, OH: Olio Press, 2000.

Mignola, M. *Hellboy: Chained Coffin & Others.* Milwaukie, OR: Dark Horse Comics, 1998.

Millar, M. *Ultimate X-Men.* New York: Marvel Books, 2002.

Miller, F. *Batman: The Dark Knight Returns.* New York: DC Comics, 1997.

Miller, F. *Daredevil Legends.* New York: Marvel Books, 1990.

Millionaire, T. *Sock Monkey: Glass Doorknob.* Milwaukie, OR: Dark Horse Maverick, 2002.

Miyazaki, H. *Castle in the Sky.* San Francisco: Viz Communications, 2003.

Miyazaki, H. *Nausicaa of the Valley of Wind.* San Francisco: Viz Communications, 1995.

Miyazaki, H. *Spirited Away.* San Francisco: Viz Communications, 2002.

Moore, A. *Watchmen.* New York: DC Comics, 1995.

Oakley, M. *Thieves and Kings: Blue Book.* Wolfville, NS: I Box Publishing, 1998.

Peter, C. *Young Justice: A League of Their Own.* New York: DC Comics, 2000.

Pini, W., and R. Pini. *Elfquest.* New York: DC Comics, 2003.

Powerpuff Girls. New York: Scholastic Books, 2002.

Robinson, J. *Starman.* New York: DC Comics, 1996.

Sacco, J. *Safe Area Gorazde.* Seattle: Fantagraphics Books, 2002.

Sakai, S. *Usagi Yojimbo.* Milwaukie, OR: Dark Horse Comics, 1999.

Samura, H. *Blade of the Immortal.* Milwaukie, OR: Dark Horse Comics, 2001.

Satrapi, M. *Persepolis: The Story of a Childhood.* New York: Pantheon Books, 2003.

Shanower, E. *Age of Bronze: A Thousand Ships.* Orange, CA: Image Comics, 2001.

Smith, J. *Bone.* Columbus, OH: Cartoon Books, 1995.

Smith, K. *Green Arrow: Quiver.* New York: DC Comics, 2003.

Soryo, F. *Mars.* Los Angeles: TokyoPop, 2002.

Spiegelman, A. *Maus.* New York: Pantheon Books, 1986.

Takahashi, R. *Inu Yasha.* San Francisco, CA: Viz Communications, 2003.

Takahashi, R. *Ranma ½.* San Francisco, CA: Viz Communications, 2002.

Takahashi, K. *Yu-Gi-Oh!* San Francisco, CA: Viz Communications, 2003.

Talbot, B. *Tale of One Bad Rat.* Milwaukie, OR: Dark Horse Comics, 1995.

Tezuka, O. *Astro Boy.* Milwaukie, OR: Dark Horse Comics, 2002.

Thompson, C. *Goodbye, Chunky Rice.* Marietta, GA: Top Shelf Productions, 2002.

Thompson, J. *Scary Godmother.* San Antonio, TX: Sirius Entertainment, 1999.

Toriyama, A. *Dragonball Z.* San Francisco, CA: Viz Communications, 2000.

Veitch, T. *Star Wars: Dark Empire.* New York: Pan Macmillan, 1995.

Waid, M. *Ruse.* Oldsmar, FL: CrossGeneration Comics, 2001.

Walt Disney Comics. Gladstone Publishing, 1990.

Watase, Y. *Fushigi Yugi*. San Francisco: Viz Communications, 2003.

Winick, J. *Pedro and Me:Friendship, Loss, and What I Learned*. New York: Henry Holt, 2000.

Yasuhiko, Y. *Joan*. Fremont, CA: ComicsOne, 2001.

Chapter 6

The Comics Journal. Seattle: Fantagraphics Books, 1976– . Monthly.

Eisner, W. *Comics & Sequential Art*. Poorhouse Press, 1994.

Eisner, W. *Graphic Storytelling& Visual Narrative*. Poorhouse Press, 1996.

McCloud, S. *Reinventing Comics: How Imagination and Technology Are Revolutionizing an Art Form*. New York: DC Comics, 2000.

McCloud, S. *Understanding Comics*. New York: Paradox Press, 1994.

Overstreet, R. *The Overstreet Comic Book Price Guide*. Timonium, MD: Gemstone Publishing, 1970– . Annual.

Weiner, S. *101 Best Graphic Novels*. New York: NBM Publishing, 2003.

Wizard: The Comics Magazine. Congers, NY: Wizard Entertainment, 1991– . Monthly.

Chapter 7

Atangan, P. *The Yellow Jar*. New York: NBM Publishing, 2002.

Eisner, W. *Moby Dick*. New York: NBM Publishing, 1998.

Eisner, W. *Sundiata: A Legend of Africa*. New York: NBM Publishing, 2002.

Gaiman, N. *The Wolves in the Walls*. New York: HarperCollins, 2003.

Gownley, J. *Amelia Rules*. Harrisburg, PA: Renaissance Press, 2001.

Kochalka, J. *Monkey vs. Robot*. Marietta, GA: Top Shelf Productions, 2000.

Kochalka, J. *Pinky & Stinky*. Marietta, GA: Top Shelf Productions, 2002.

Medley, L. *Castle Waiting: Curse of the Brambly Hedge*. Columbus, OH: Olio Press, 2000.

Robin, T., and L. Trondheim. *Li'l Santa*. New York: NBM Publishing, 2002.

Shanower, E. *Age of Bronze: A Thousand Ships*. Orange, CA: Image Comics, 2001.

Usui, Y. *Crayon ShinChan*. Fremont, CA: ComicsOne, 2002.

Index

For Reference

Not to be taken from this room